The CHANGING FACE of BRITAIN -from the Air

The
CHANGING
FACE
of
BRITAIN
-from the Air

Text by Leslie Gardiner
Foreword by Asa Briggs

Michael Joseph

MICHAEL JOSEPH LTD

Published by the Penguin Group
27 Wrights Lane, London W8 5TZ, England
Viking Penguin Inc., 40 West 23rd Street, New York, New York 10010, USA
Penguin Books Australia Ltd, Ringwood, Victoria, Australia
Penguin Books Canada Ltd, 2801 John Street, Markham, Ontario, Canada L3R 1B4
Penguin Books (NZ) Ltd, 182-190 Wairau Road, Auckland 10, New Zealand

Penguin Books Ltd. Registered Offices: Harmondsworth, Middlesex, England

First published in Great Britain 1989

Typeset in Great Britain by Lineage Ltd, Watford, Herts
Originated in Hong Kong by Regent Publishing Services
Printed in Hong Kong

A CIP catalogue record for this book is available from the British Library

ISBN 0 7181 2874 5

Photo enlargements
All the pictures in this book are available as photographic enlargements from the
original negatives. The monochrome photographs were selected from hundreds of
thousands in the Aerofilms Library.

Free proofs and price list from:

Aerofilms Ltd, Gate Studios, Station Road,
Borehamwood, Herts, WD6 1EJ

Contents

Foreword

This book is essential reading – and viewing – for anyone who wishes to discover how and why Britain has changed during the last half century. The pace of change has varied, and the change has often been controversial. There is no doubt, however, about the result. The face of Britain has been transformed.

Within these pages there is unique and fascinating evidence. The photographs are not just bird's-eye views, appealing though these have always been through the ages, but human vistas stimulating thought and argument about our recent past. What has disappeared is just as revealing as what is new. Some landmarks have gone, some whole districts have been transformed. The country as a whole has new arteries as a result of wide-reaching developments in transportation. They were already well advanced before the word 'environment' came into general use – significantly along with the word 'heritage' – during the 1970s.

Television has turned viewing into the main national pastime. 'Learning to look' outside the home is still backward. Even before television, however, aerial photography, pioneered between the two world wars, had made it possible – in a phrase of Maurice Beresford, a distinguished economic historian – to comprehend detail as a unity. And even before the First World War, before the aeroplane was invented, the question of what you can actually see from the air and how it differs from what you can see on the ground had been raised by pioneers of the balloon.

Maps, of course, are necessary complements. So also is the commentary attached to the photographs in this book. Comparing before and after is always interesting, sometimes exciting. These are pictures that will stimulate the imagination, although different readers will have their own ideas about which particular pictures stimulate their imagination most.

Asa Briggs
Worcester College, Oxford
1989

Introduction

'We see nothing until we truly understand it,' wrote John Constable, the landscape painter. And so we accompany our aerial views of Britain and Ireland – ancient and modern, town and country, coastal and landward – with a commentary which aims to set the historical frame round each pair of pictures and show reasons for the changes which have occurred between the earlier scene and the later.

Our old pictures go back 30, 50, sometimes nearly 70 years, to the dawn of aerial photography. New pictures were taken in 1987 and 1988.

In his *English Journey* (1934), J.B. Priestley saw three lands. There was the Olde Englande of village green and yew tree, parson and squire, medieval streets and cathedrals. Intruding on that was the sprawl of 19th-century industry, of sham-Gothic churches and chapels and 'thousands of little houses all alike'. Then, after 1918, came suburbia and cheap motor cars, adorning the land with arterial roads, by-passes, road houses, filling stations, bungalows, Woolworths and 'everything given away for cigarette cards'.

Cameos of those three lands are plentiful in our older pictures. In the new, a fourth aspect is disclosed. Motorways make the arterial roads look like country lanes. Shopping malls and supermarkets reduce the modest chain-stores of the 1930s to corner-shop status. The bungalows and 'little houses all alike' have mushroomed into high-rise glass-and-concrete tower blocks. The medieval streets are pedestrian precincts. The village green is sometimes – not always – overrun by a 'new town' or a bleak municipal estate. The broad-leaved woodland is sometimes – not always – in retreat before regiments of fir and spruce. Hedgerows, ditches and coppices, anything which gets in the way of farm machinery, are sometimes – not always – swept away and the old patchwork quilt of a mixed farming economy becomes one huge self-coloured bedspread from here to the horizon.

The parson must still be around – we can see his church. Many of our then-and-now comparisons proclaim the durability of churches. They frequently stand alone in a wasteland levelled by World War II air raids, looking exactly the same as they did fifty years ago. Why should they not? Some of them have been like that for 700 years. How many of our multi-million-pound tower blocks will be standing 70 years from now, let alone 700?

Yet much has changed for the better. E.P. Thompson warns against 'the enormous condescension of posterity', but we can look back on old scenes with pity as well as nostalgia. Those good old bad old days. Old-time pictures of inner-city life encompass a physical and spiritual desolation hardly imaginable even in the ghettoes of today. The canopies of black smoke are gone; there are green spaces within five minutes of everyone's home; in town centres you walk from shop to shop, not across streets roaring with juggernauts but across coloured flagstones dotted with flower-beds and box-trees in tubs.

Those agricultural monsters which have devoured the hedgerows and copses have also devoured much of the drudgery that went with farming. The rivers which were corridors of dirty warehouses and coils of rusty wire are now lined with footpaths and gardens. Unsightly quarries blossom into watersports centres, decrepit fishing ports are sparkling yacht marinas, concert halls rise from old slums and the disused railway or canal towpath is a joggers' route or a cycle track.

Britain and Ireland are still fascinating and beautiful countries – 'a whole world of things very memorable', as Leland said – and quite unlike any other. If we are not happier and healthier here than we were, then we ought to be.

The aerial view is a living map, which exaggerates some features and diminishes others. Someone's gravelled backyard may be startlingly obtrusive. Look straight down on Salisbury spire and you see nothing unless it is casting a shadow. Ridged roofs denote older factories as a rule, flat roofs generally belong to cinemas, supermarkets or modern factories – the best guide to their importance is often the size of adjacent car parks.

The greens and bunkers of golf courses show up well; so do school playgrounds and playing fields, though the school buildings may be hard to locate. Railways seem to slink through the landscape, avoiding the camera's eye. The courses of unseen rivers may be traced through wavering lines of trees. Ships stand out clearly, as do the barrel-roofed market halls of northern towns. Footpaths on land and shallows in the sea are nearly always well defined. From the air you may observe the palimpsests of archaeology and the long-erased shapes of fields and abandoned rights of way.

The authors have been grateful for information generously supplied by the planning departments of various towns and cities, particularly Manchester, Derby, Oldham, Leeds and Birmingham; by district libraries, notably East Lothian; and by the local studies departments of city libraries. Much has been learned from the series of topographical books which over the past twenty years or so have covered almost all the cities and regions of Britain and Ireland – surely no other countries in the world offer a richer or better written collection of landscape literature. From the Introduction to one of them (*The Hertfordshire Landscape* by Lionel M. Munby, Hodder & Stoughton 1977) we borrow our message to the reader:

'We have tried to say what we have to say simply and without too much academic pretension, for any worthwhile look at a landscape must be for all readers and not merely for the specialist.'

Leslie and Adrian Gardiner
Gifford, East London
1989

1961

Milton Keynes

Here is a Bedfordshire village sitting quietly at a storm centre, hardly aware of what is going on around it. In 27 years, between the *old* and *new pictures*, there have been only minor changes to the village itself. The formerly gravelled roads are properly surfaced. The unsightly quarry (*new picture*, left) came with the building of the M1 motorway (upper right); but the next-door farmhouse survives, as do the parish church (centre, in trees) and some thatched buildings (lower centre). (We are looking west towards Newport Pagnell (right) and Wolverton (left).)

Also to the west begins the business section of the new Milton Keynes (*new town picture*); and what a contrast. This marvel of modern urban design was established from 1967 onwards as the first custom-built 'new town'. It was a symbol of affluent and optimistic times, a realization of the cleaner, healthier Britain which all political parties had been promising since the 1945 General Election. The planners marked out 40 square miles, overlapping the market town of

Bletchley, the railway centre of Wolverton and the ancient site of Stony Stratford, and sketched in housing and industrial estates for 250,000 people.

A Californian surrealism informed the plan. Parks, avenues and landscaped pools were created. Millions of trees were planted. A bold traffic system provided freeways through the open-plan residential and business sections. 'Drive to work at 50 m.p.h.' was the slogan. (People complained that, after moving in, they could no longer afford a car, but the *new town picture* suggests that many have solved that problem.)

Mirror-glass civic offices, with central library and art gallery alongside, are in the centre of the *new town picture*, beside the roof-top pool. City Park (top centre) accommodates a huge shopping complex – and 6,000 free parking spaces to go with it. Woven among the rectilinear carriageways are labyrinths of cycle tracks and footpaths.

In the residential section you buy a plot and build as you like, which makes for an interesting confusion of angles and styles.

The Open University is sited near another park and lake (far right, out of picture). Beside B-shaped Willen Lake (top left) stands the western world's first Peace Pagoda (white with black spire, between left edge of lake and Grand Union Canal), built by Japanese Buddhist monks.

Now 20 years old, Milton Keynes has a population of about 110,000, the majority locally employed. For industry and commerce it is strategically located: half-way house between London and Birmingham, handy for the motor manufacturers of Coventry and Luton, the cement and electrical engineering works of Rugby, the steel at Corby, the leather at Northampton and the bricks in Bedfordshire. It bestrides the main rail, canal and road routes between south and north – before a stone was laid, the village from which it took its name was trembling to the thunder of traffic on the M1 motorway (*new picture*, upper right). As a design for future living, Milton Keynes may be considered promising.

Ealing

This is where John Betjeman saw from his Harrow hill 'the harbour lights of Perivale' in a mysterious twilit London. Not nearly as built-up as they promised to be in our *old picture* where the new Western Avenue was about to cross the Grand Union canal, areas of Ealing ('Queen of the Suburbs') like Perivale and Greenford retain a distinctly small-town atmosphere (*new picture* top) and, where Western Avenue runs, the land is still ripe for development. Ealing still boasts 97 churches and 51 green spaces, counting golf courses.

Western Avenue (A40) began as a relief road for congested traffic on the Great West Road: even in the 1920s, Hounslow and Brentford were notorious bottlenecks. The new urban parkway thrust into the scene like a brash transatlantic intruder – an image reinforced when Hoover, Kodak, Gillette, Osram and others lined the road with factories, introducing Britain to household goods and labour-saving devices with which American families were already familiar. In its street names – Uneeda, Rockware, Purex – Greenford commemorates some of the products. The brilliant art-deco Hoover factory and the highly 'contemporary' Firestone building (demolished in 1980 despite a preservation order) were appropriate embellishments to the clean-cut lines and intersections of the dual-carriage racetrack.

Since 1945 some big home-grown companies have raised extra capital and cut overheads by selling their West End sites and migrating to the 'Sunrise Belt' in West Middlesex and Berkshire. Rank Xerox, I.C.I. and British Aluminium took this route in the 1970s. But pre-war forecasts that Western Avenue, between White City, Ealing and Hillingdon, would become the grand canyon of Britain's light-industrial base have curiously remained unfulfilled. Green sites abound. The canal is a rustic waterway. Several major firms have departed. Hoover's celebrated facade survives, but the factory was closed some years ago, with the loss of 11,000 jobs.

1934

1931

Great Missenden

Quietly lodged on the London-Aylesbury highway, entirely surrounded by farms, this community at the date of our *old picture* merited the description applied by John Leland nearly four centuries earlier: 'a pretty thoroughfare but no market town'. The High Street (*old picture*, centre) proved inadequate for through traffic on an increasingly busy route and in 1950 Great Missenden acquired its bypass (*new picture* foreground).

The bypass separated the community from its parish church of Sts Peter and Paul (*both pictures*, lower centre). Since the church stands 50 feet above the new road, the access footbridge carries worshippers straight across the traffic and into the porch.

In the era of promiscuous ribbon development along the radial roads from London, most Buckinghamshire villages suffered from a fever of speculative building. Bungalows sprinted along the highways, close-knit townships were fringed with villas in the stockbroker-Tudor style. For a country location less than an hour from London by road or rail, Great Missenden has come off lightly. Most new building has been sited discreetly in woodland, in the direction of Prestwood (*new picture*, top centre). The population is no more than 10,000 – most of them to be found thronging the still-picturesque High Street on a Saturday morning. If Leland returned, he would call the place 'a pretty market town but no thoroughfare'.

The neighbouring countryside preserves its soft Chilterns character: farmland, hedgerows, woodland, springy turf. Rooted in the chalk they love, the beech trees (*both pictures*, foreground) stand like sentinels, watchful of the landscape, seemingly more enduring than tarmac, bricks and mortar. The scene is parklike, though Buckinghamshire's famous stately homes – Hughenden, Chenies, Chequers, Little Gaddesden – are out of sight. The one noteworthy building here (*both pictures*, left centre) is fake-Gothic Missenden Abbey, now an adult education centre.

1959

Hollywood

Behind our pictures is a war story – a war of attrition, a bulging
conurbation's relentless pressure on its surroundings. Hollwood,
situated where rural Arden met Birmingham, was a district of
scattered farmsteads and small, irregular, hedged fields shaped by
piecemeal enclosure from the forests and heaths of Saxon times (*old
picture* left, bottom and lower right). Farms had names like Hollytree,
Yewtree and Woodleaf; also Kingswood and Hawkesley, this having
been a royal manor and hunting ground. Silver Street, the medieval
salt road from Droitwich (bottom left) passed through.

By 1959, above and below the Gay Hill golf clubhouse (*old picture*
centre at road junction), crescents of modern houses had gained a
foothold. Close-packed terraces along the A435, the old Alcester road
(centre to top left) lay in the shadows of the Druids Heath tower
blocks beyond the Birmingham boundary.

Simm's Lane (bottom centre left) had had a small housing scheme
in the 1930s. It was enlarged in 1952 and again in 1964 and 1967.
Trueman's Heath (*new picture* bottom centre right) was also built up in
three stages between 1963 and 1966. Meantime, battles rages over the
area south of Maypole Lane (*old picture* top right to top left). In 1959
Birmingham applied to build 14,000 houses and two industrial estates.
Hollywood got the scheme thrown out, but the Housing Minister

(Henry Brooke) changed his mind and allowed partial development. His successor (Charles Hill) accepted Hollywood's indignant appeal and stopped it. In 1964 Birmingham tried again and a tough, expensive enquiry ended in her favour – but a change of government saved Hollywood. In 1969 the city attacked once more and was repulsed.

For Hollywood these were Pyrrhic victories. Piecemeal enclosure (as in the Middle Ages) won all the land west of the Alcester road (*new picture* left) – not for agriculture but for housing.

Gay Hill was spared. It is amazing how golf courses manage to resist the developers. The fields to the east (*new picture* right) are also reprieved, at least until Birmingham's next application for 'overspill' planning permission. They are almost all that is left of the great elm forest of Arden, which once spread over three counties.

A consolation for Hollywoodians, who mostly commute to Birmingham and Bromsgrove, is that industry is banned. And the township is once again lightly trafficked, because the 1968 bypass (left, out of *pictures*) speeds commuters and the high-density commercial flow of the region between the 'new town' of Redditch and the road network of Birmingham.

1952

Glenrothes

On the rim of the fertile Howe (hollow) of Fife, along the wooded valleys of the River Leven and Rothes Burn (*new picture*, extreme left), there were paper mills and a few country houses and cottages. Mining villages of the Fife coalfield were scattered round about. The scene began to change dramatically in 1947, when they chose the place for a 'new town'. From the name of the stream they called it Glenrothes.

The *old picture* shows the first part of the 'new town' under construction; the larger part is out of sight, to the right and bottom of *both pictures*. As one of the very first, and most northerly, of all 'new towns', Glenrothes with its pre-cast concrete semi-detached houses and low tenements looks harsh and dour, not a vast improvement on the rows of miners' cottages round about. But its layout and amenities were considered luxurious.

The now-matured Glenrothes of our *new picture* benefits from abundant tree growth and some variations in building styles. More individualistic housing has appeared (bottom left). Shopping areas, schools and public gardens break up the monotonous grey terraces ('deserts wi' windaes', a Scottish comedian called them). The main Dundee-Kirkcaldy road, going to the Firth of Forth (*new picture*, top), intersects other cross-country routes and rings the 35,000 population with large traffic islands.

The 'new town' was built for miners in a post-war boom which never came. Within 20 years every Fife coalfield but one had been closed. But Tullis Russell's paper mills prospered and American electronics firms arrived (*new picture*, upper right) to establish the manufacture and assembly of components for computers, communications systems and space satellites.

1924

Burnt Oak

Someone tired, it seems, of human society, is building himself a fort-like refuge in a lonely landscape (*old picture*). Judging by the *new picture*, he has picked the wrong spot. Sixty years on he sits at a busy road and rail intersection (centre). The clover-leaf of a planned community of 20,000 people is arranged around him.

Just off the Watling Street (A5) (bottom left, out of sight) and last stop before the terminus on the Underground's Northern Line to Edgware, the fort-like refuge – actually the Tube station – was the first building in Burnt Oak, though only nine miles from central London. It was opened in October 1924, five months after our *old picture* was taken. Among Tube stations it was unique: instead of following the population out of London, it led the population. Where other Tube stations (about 250 of them) sprouted in response to the public's needs, Burnt Oak was deliberately set up to attract builders to the idea of a housing estate in a rural setting and to persuade Londoners to live in it. The *new*

picture shows how successful the scheme turned out to be. It also shows how neat and pleasant, at least from the air, is a suburb conceived and built as a whole, as this was under the Greater London Council, compared with the sad piecemeal sprawl which disfigures the capital's approaches elsewhere.

Burnt Oak station, straddling a Northern Line which here runs on the surface, is outwardly little changed. It stands beside a major road, Mill Hill to a Watling Street junction, which was only a footpath in our *old picture*. It represents a landmark in the orgy of progress which characterized London transport from the beginning of this century – from horse-buses to motor-buses and trams, from steam trains to electric trains and the proliferation of Underground lines.

Each transport innovation enabled London's workers to live farther out from the centre, transformed outer suburbs into inner suburbs and led progressively to the phenomena of dormitory towns, satellite towns, overspill towns and 'new towns'.

1930

Bere Alston

The country lanes (*old picture*) were smooth, narrow and white with chalk dust; not much stirred by traffic. Devon was tough country for motor cars in those days of two-wheel brakes, vulnerable tyres and boiling radiators. Afterwards, its up-hill-and-down-dale roads with 1000-year-old hedgerows arching over them (*old picture* top centre) became the congested touring ground of holiday motorists and excursion buses.

The roads are tarmac now (*new picture*) and Bere Alston has a web of streets. The village has quadrupled its population but is still a compact community with well-defined boundaries. Post-1945 housing, including the cottage block which has gone up on the garden allotments (*new picture* right of centre) does not clash seriously with the older houses on the main street: local stone and traditional building methods still rule. Small-holdings and farmhouses remain intact, though hemmed in. Traffic is still relatively light.

The surrounding countryside is a corner of Devon-next-to-Cornwall, almost isolated in the convolutions of the Tamar and Tavy (top right) rivers. Foreigners – that is to say, anyone from beyond Tavistock – knew Bere Alston as the junction for a slow train trip across the Tamar into Cornwall, a route as serpentine and idyllic as that of the river itself. That line is closed, but on another there are nine trains a day to Plymouth and nine in the other direction for Gunnislake near Tavistock. This helps explain Bere Alston's expansion: you no longer live there to work there. But farming is still important on the chalk tableland, where once they ploughed with eight oxen and now, on broader fields, do twice the job in a fifth of the time with tractors. In the frost-free hollows a few small farmers still grow early daffodils, violets and broccoli and road-freight them to south-of-England city markets.

1922

Welsh Harp

Half close your eyes and our *old picture* resembles an 18th-century
topographical engraving. London's suburban growth, very much of
the 20th century, has absorbed the pastoral scene into populous Brent,
symbol of controversial urban politics. Only the railway (upper left)
and the Welsh Harp reservoir (top) appear common to both pictures.
Upper left in the *new picture* the Leeds-London motorway (M1) now
accompanies the Bedford-St Pancras railway towards the capital.

In the foreground, the houses and factories of Colindale spread
south to a medium- and high-rise flat complex near the water's edge.
On the extreme right they skirt the last open spaces to join hands with
Neasden's drab industry, rail sidings and cooling towers. Until this
century Hendon (*both pictures*, upper left) was a mere group of
hamlets. It is now a borough of 300,000 inhabitants, and a new
shopping centre near the junction of the M1 and North Circular Road
(top left) occupies 52 acres. Actor-manager David Garrick, lord of

Hendon manor 1756-1778, would not find familiar landmarks now;
nor would 1920s resident Evelyn Waugh, who trudged two miles daily
into Hampstead to get a more refined postmark on his letters.

The Brent river and the Silk stream (lackadaisical then, firmly
disciplined now) were dammed to form the 350-acre reservoir and to
feed the Regent's Canal. Upper right from the water crossing in the
new picture, Cool Oak Lane has lost its oak trees and gained a few
garden centres and sports grounds. The Welsh Harp – named for a
long-vanished pub, not, as some believe, for its triangular shape – has
a history of sports and recreations: its waters cover a once-notorious
fairground, described by a Victorian diarist as 'low, vulgar and
commonplace to a degree'. Now it is lively at weekends with
speedboat racing. Its shores are no longer a bird sanctuary but many
waterfowl, unaware of this, continue to nest in increasingly noisy and
hazardous surroundings.

1929

Crawley

No wonder the railway looms large in aerial shots of Crawley; no wonder there is ample parking for passengers at the station (*new picture*, bottom right): 600 trains pass through Crawley every weekday. Rapid communication with the capital helped attract new residents and spread a promiscuous growth of semi-detached houses and bungalows along the Sussex lanes soon after the First World War (*old picture*, bottom left and top right). Such dwellings, no less than the old grey church (*both pictures*, centre right) and a few well-built farmhouses and thatched manor houses (*old picture* foreground), are now the period pieces of a greatly expanded population centre.

Two German balloonists, adrift over Sussex in 1917, wrote of their astonishment at the tiny meadows, the doll's-house villages, the manicured hedgerows and the general miniaturization of the English countryside. They floated over Crawley, a market township on the Brighton road, set amid deep grazing and rich arable soil. It was a pony-and-trap society then: 'What traveller will seek,' said the guidebook, 'to evade our little hostelry, whose host always appears at the guest's arrival, in one hand a gallon bottle of gin and in the other a wicker basket filled with thin slices of gingerbread?' Contrast that with your welcome today at hotels of the multinational chains which have overrun Gatwick up the road and Crawley itself.

Still a civilized spot in a lush landscape and only 30 miles from London, the town could hardly avoid being, between the wars, a preferred location for the city gent and his family. But in 1951 London's acute housing shortage necessitated the dispersal of a million citizens, of whom 65,000 came to a 'new town' at Crawley.

To the right of the railway (new picture) Crawley has the customary 'new town' features of shopping precincts, blocks of flats (of conservative design) and industrial sites; but the major developments have been to the west (out of *picture*, on left). Industry is fairly hygienic: light engineering, plastics, electronics, furniture. Several commercial firms, driven out of London by high rates and rents, have set up their head offices here. The biggest local employer by far is the British Airports Authority at Gatwick. Only four miles away, Crawley catches the crumbs of the prosperity which ten million passengers bring to the airport every year.

Meopham

'A delightful walk it was … cooled by the light wind and enlivened by the songs of birds … long vistas of stately elms and oaks appeared … 'If this,' said Mr Pickwick, looking about him, 'if this were the place to which all who are troubled with our friend's complaint came, I fancy their old attachment to this world would very soon return' – 'I think so too,' said Mr Winkle.'

Cobham, to which the Pickwickians were returning, is near the upper right edge of *both pictures*. Other villages (middle foreground to top left) include Meopham (pronounced Meppam) Green, Meopham, Hook Green and Istead Rise. Kent is a county of hamlets and villages. Where the North Downs slope northward to Gravesend (*new picture*, top), they are thickly strewn.

As in most agricultural regions, some fields have been enlarged (*new picture*, bottom and left) and some woodland pushed aside or realigned to maximize crop acreages (left foreground and upper centre). Between windbreaks (*old picture*, right foreground), exotic vegetables were probably grown for the London markets. They appear not to have done well – or perhaps campers (*new picture*, bottom right) pay better than asparagus.

Meopham village preserves its historic triangular cricket pitch and pavilion (*old picture*, centre), with pubs on two sides and, standing back, an old windmill with a fresh coat of paint (*new picture*, upper centre, edge of shadow). By admitting only a few new houses along the Green, this patch of rural Kent celebrates its escape from the Abercrombie Plan of 1944, under which it was designated a 'new town' site. Eventually judged unsuitable, it was included 20 years later in London's extended green belt.

1946

1950

Merstham

The London orbital motorway M25 (*new picture*, lower left to top), the M23 Caterham-Crawley motorway (upper left to right) and British Rail's Brighton line (lower left to right) cut deep swathes in the Surrey landscape. What may look like 'creeping suburbia' has crept fast indeed in 30-odd years, leaping the railway and taking possession of a good four square miles of coppice and meadow. New building and new lines of communication have not, however, disturbed the character of the countryside as much as they might have done. The M25 has spared the Pilgrims' Way (*old picture*, left) and the ridge of the North Downs (left) remains virtually intact. The slopes are more rustic now than they were 200 years ago, when pure limestone was quarried and sent up to London to make mortar and cement for the Georgian squares and terraces of Regent's Park and Belgravia.

Neither the quarries nor the Surrey Iron Railway of 1805 (the world's first), horse-drawn with stone from Merstham to Wandsworth, intruded on the simple peasant life. Cobbett, on a rural ride of 1832 found nothing more noteworthy at Merstham than 'a field of cabbages'. A century later, when the village (bottom of *old picture*, far right) had a proper railway, Seymour Hicks and Ellaline Terriss set up home there. They starred in a J.M. Barrie hit and Merstham renamed their lane 'Quality Street'.

Dramatic transformations followed the London County Council's choice of Merstham in the 1950s as its first 'out-county estate' – a sort of overspill township, built to fixed limits with due consideration for the natural environment: a township designed for those who looked forward to a country walk or a bit of gardening after a day in a stuffy London office. Strategically it was an excellent decision: no one could have foreseen a major motorway interchange on Merstham's doorstep. Whether ease of communication and increased land values outweigh the noise pollution from Britain's busiest speedway is a question only the residents can answer.

1935

Borehamwood

More than half a million people have moved into Hertfordshire this century, most of them since 1945. All had to live somewhere. *New picture* (left) shows a corner of a town which the London County Council created in the early 1950s round the villages of Borehamwood and Elstree.

The plans had been on the drawing board for 20 years. Our *old picture* is a typical scene of what then passed, in the Home Counties, for rustic seclusion. Inevitably an arterial road passed through, and where you found an arterial road you generally found a Jacobean-style inn or (in the terminology of the 1930s) a 'roadhouse'. This place (upper centre) is a hotel called the Thatched Barn. Its thatched roofs and restrained half-timbering look less offensively 'period' than most.

And it has survived virtually intact (*new*

picture, centre right). Judging by the way
its already ample accommodation has
expanded (back of hotel), it has also
prospered. They now call it Thatcher's.

We are looking at the eastern edge of
Borehamwood. The main road (*both pictures*,
bottom centre to upper right) is the A1, the
Great North Road, coming out of London
and leading towards Potters Bar and Hatfield.
Back in 1868, it was the opening of a local
railway station on the St Pancras-Bedford line
which made Borehamwood a real village.
Now the realignment of the A1, as well as the
building of the out-county estate, has made it
a real town. In the 1950s most residents
worked in London: the only local employers
were Elstree film studios (*new picture*, top
left). Now there are factories and businesses
of various kinds – including Aerofilms.

Antrim

At the date of our *old picture* there were scarcely more motor-cars in the whole of County Antrim than are now parked at the supermarket and the D.I.Y. shop (*new picture*, upper centre and right) and in the streets and gardens (lower and bottom right) of the smart residential developments along Six Mile Water at Antrim. The small county town, an overgrown village by English standards, has spread out in all directions. The new main road and its offshoots (left, top to bottom; left to upper right) seem to enclose Antrim protectively and to emphasize the defensive qualities of its situation. The town was bitterly fought over in 1649 and again in 1798.

1926

Clumps of birch and poplar (*old picture*, foreground) have been sacrificed for housing, but the beautiful stand of timber in Antrim Park (*old picture*, upper left; *new picture*, top), mostly cedars, firs, silver birches and poplars, has survived. The Dutch garden and the ornamental waters survive too (top left) but the castle, seat of Lord Masserene and Ferrard, was accidentally burned down in 1922. Old Antrim was made up of typical linen-spinners' cottages. Despite expansion and modernization, the main-street houses retain their clean, wholesome, frugal character, as do the Court House (left end of street, with clock tower) and the Protestant church (right).

Antrim has become a commuter town. Only 16 miles from Belfast, formerly a weary day-long journey, it is now within minutes of the Northern Ireland capital, thanks to the motorways M1 and M2 which are cross-connected by the A26 highway, snaking through Antrim *en route* (*new picture*, left). Aldergrove, the airport for Belfast, only four miles south, also provides jobs. But the town has a life of its own. Its lake fishing is well organized, it has a People's Theatre, and a summer theatre in the woods. It may have to become a centre of industry too: in 1987 they discovered lignite (half coal, half peat) on the Lough Neagh shore: important news for energy-starved Ireland.

1926

Carrick-on-Shannon

'You'll have seen that film, *A Bridge Too Far*' says the man at the boatyard. 'Well, this is A Bridge Too Narrow.' He is warning us about the first hazard (*old picture*, centre left; *new picture*, upper left edge) on the voyage down the Shannon. That trip of 140 miles, the longest inland voyage in the British Isles, covers eight Irish counties, two large lakes, countless sweeping bends and midstream islands, and six locks. It is an ordeal for those who have never been afloat before, or have only cruised on canals.

But many come to Carrick-on-Shannon to do it. That has been the biggest single factor in the transformation of a lackadaisical Leitrim village into a hinterland marina for 150 boats, a centre for regattas and aquatic sports, an accommodation area offering rented cottages and farmhouse holidays. The horse-and-cart society of yesteryear (*old picture*, on bridge), where desultory fishing (also on bridge) was the sole recreation for 800 inhabitants, is now a thriving population with two hotels and a score of entrepreneurs who not only hire out cabin cruisers but also launch, fuel, service and repair the boats that some visitors bring with them. On Carrick's main street, between June and September, you hear the accents of all parts of Britain and of some parts of the Continent and the U.S.A. too. In the old days a foreigner was the object of profound suspicion.

A sign of good times is the number of beautiful modern, clearly architect-designed dwelling houses (left foreground, for example). Carrick has expanded gracefully, which is something few villages and fewer tourist centres do. Clean white stone, characteristic of these north-western counties of the Republic, makes even garages and grocery shops look handsome. By comparison, the village's historic nucleus near the Shannon bridge (*new picture*, upper left) appears slummy, a relic of a bog-trotting Ireland almost vanished. Yet it is a charming little Percy French cameo, where you buy lettuce at the post office and newspapers at the butcher's; where the three-coach Sligo train's arrival is the event of the day, where the pub is also the funeral parlour and where, when you say 'Good evening' at around 7pm, the inhabitants answer 'Goodnight'.

1948

Ploughing near St Neot's, Cambridgeshire

The light plough in our *old picture*, needing only one horse, drills soft earth for potatoes.

In the *new picture* one field (right) has been ploughed and rolled flat. In the other (on left) a tractor ploughs the stubble under (pale strip, top to bottom). A characteristic retinue of seagulls, often seen far inland, follows the plough.

Veteran countrymen indulge a sentimental nostalgia for the old labour-intensive, horse-drawn ploughing days, the serenity and slow pace, the affectionate relationship of man and animal, the pride in a straight furrow. The horse started at a touch on a cold morning – more than you could say for the diesel tractor. Horses manured the ground as they went and planted their hooves in a pattern ideal for irrigation when rainwater filled the holes. Champions of mechanization say the tractor does a better and faster job. The modern all-purpose tractor can be used with sophisticated equipment for a tremendous variety of tasks. The farmer can lock it up in a shed and go away for his holidays, which he could never do with horses.

In 1910 the British farm horse population reached one million, the highest in history. Thirty years later there were half a million, and 65,000 tractors. Since 1960 working horses have been so few that statistics show them as nil. The number of tractors is steady at about 450,000 but their power and versatility increase all the time. Rising labour costs and difficulty in attracting young people to agriculture tempt farmers to invest more and more in tractors and tractor-mounted implements. Even small farms may keep several tractors, each of which works 800-1000 hours every year.

The ploughman of our *new picture* works in comfort, whatever the climate. His vehicle has a cushioned seat with folding armrests in an air-conditioned safety cab. It has an electric starter, four-wheel drive, a gearbox with 16 forward speeds, power-assisted steering and a differential lock to stop one wheel slipping while the other bears more of the load – the dangerous defect of earlier tractors when canted in a furrow or riding a slope. With his power-shift gears and manual-shuttle reverse controls and a dozen implement-linkage and pick-up switches grouped in consoles at his right elbow, the tractor-driver manipulates an array of instruments which would not disgrace a Rolls Royce – and he is in charge of a vehicle which may cost just as much.

1947

Harvesting near Berkhamsted, Herts

In the *old picture* the countryside is stippled with wheat-sheaves which have been reaped and bound and then stooked' by hand, eight sheaves to a pyramidical stook, for drying. Horse-drawn wagons (centre and right) carry them to the corn-stack which, when built, will be thatched against the August rains. Later on, the steam-driven thresher will come round, or the wheat will be transported to a stationary thresher at the farm.

In the *new picture* a combine harvester does 20 men's work in a fraction of the time – cutting the wheat, separating the grain, chopping and throwing out the stalks and laying them in a neat carpet over the field where they will be ploughed back into the soil. At

intervals another vehicle will run alongside, taking on board a load of grain to be scientifically aired at the farm's grain-drier. Drifting dust behind the combine indicates that they have chosen a good day for harvesting; but rainy or windy weather matters less nowadays because the machinery is so efficient and the operation so swift.

Animal power, scythe and sickle, gleaners like figures from a Bible story ... all have vanished from the modern arable farm. Chemicals have greatly increased crop yields and farms which in great-grandfather's day employed 70 men and women now manage with two or three.

1935

New Holland

'Hardly a tree to be seen, all the hedges gone, they'd plough the flipping road up if they could' – lament of the Humberside yeoman. There never was much tree cover, but the variegated acres, managed by generations of farming families, gave life and character to the flatlands which slide imperceptibly into the North Sea. Our *new picture's* 600-acre potato fields incorporate a score of old plantations and meadows apiece. Here on the Humber's south shore the removal of copses and hedges and a few trees (*old picture*, centre) has emphasized the billiard-table geography of coastal Lincolnshire. From a bedroom window, the heavy fields are a calm green sea from the eye to the horizon.

For brief periods in spring and early summer the land does take on a coat of many colours. These are the fringes of bulb country, enjoying more sunshine and less rain than other parts and here early potatoes, kale, seed wheat, sugar beet, roses and sweet peas are grown.

Cursed with shallow water and ferocious tides, New Holland (*both pictures*, bottom left) could never have become a deepwater port like Hull (*new picture*, top left). Its chief link with the world was the coal-fired paddle-steamer *Lincoln Castle* the only vehicle ferry on 50 miles of Humber estuary – but the £90 million Humber Bridge, four miles upstream, severed that link in 1981. Hull grabbed the boat on its retirement and it is now a floating restaurant, moored under the new bridge on the north side, at Hessle.

1949

Pilgrims' Way

Both pictures are splendid evocations of what, to jaded Londoners, is the essence of rural England: the Channel-facing escarpment of the North Downs; and at its foot The Weald of Kent.

   Across The Weald (centre and right) the 'garden of England' was more of a kitchen garden, sprinkled with orchards. Now it has given way to large-scale arable cultivation. The hedges are uprooted, the meadows steam-rollered into uniformity and the farms measured in thousands, not hundreds, of acres. When ploughs venture near the escarpment they leave a white wake: this was where G.K. Chesterton, fumbling in his pocket for a lost piece of chalk, realized he was sitting on the biggest piece of chalk in the world. Beech, oak and wild cherry – trees which love the chalk subsoil – have spread downhill (*new picture* left) and modern pilgrims on the Pilgrims' Way (*old picture* centre foreground to upper centre) walk through tunnels of leaves.

When the Romans were in Britain The Weald was *Anderida*, the 'untrodden place'. Along a North Downs trackway came Wessex merchants with wool and corn, bound for the Continent. After the murder of Thomas a'Beckett (1170), when Canterbury became the chief place of English pilgrimage, the faithful of the western counties trod a parallel path, a little lower down the escarpment, on the edge of the swamps and murky forests.

   This was the Pilgrims' Way. Probably more people walk it now than at any time in its history. The Countryside Commission has combined the Pilgrims' Way of the Middle Ages with the trackway of the Roman era to create a waymarked long-distance footpath. Steep sections are provided with steps and handrails. It is called the North Downs Way, it runs (roughly) from Farnham (Surrey) to Dover and it is 140 miles long. The section shown here is the steady descent to the Medway Gap, 55 miles from journey's end.

1934

River Avon

Robert Herrick the poet (1591-1674), vicar of Dean Prior near the
headwaters of the Avon (*both pictures*, upper right), complained of
'this dull Devonshire'. He could hardly have meant the landscape, but
if he did he would find it duller today. The kaleidoscope of farmland,
annually rotated, is gradually being erased (compare the *old* and *new*
pictures, left centre and upper right). Oilseed rape, the new yellow
peril, a successful invader of farming land all over Britain, has gained
its foothold on the Avon's banks (*new picture*, centre right); but this
region of Devon chiefly sows, fertilizes and reaps the traditional corn
and root crops. The individual smallholder, scything his steep half-
acre, is only a memory now. His humble homestead, one of those
which have thickly dotted the Devon landscape since medieval times,
is also under threat as domestic agriculture gives way to commercial
management.

The Avon, one of four British Avons – the word means simply
'river' – rises on Dartmoor and is dammed to form a reservoir which

supplies the environs of Plymouth to the west and Torbay to the east.
Thereafter, all the way to its mouth on Bigbury Bay (*both pictures,*
bottom) it is a sinuous trout stream flowing serenely among spring
bluebells, tall summer grass and woodland. In its 40-mile course it
negotiates hamlets but no towns.

At its mouth the clean shingly sands of the estuary have been
discovered by picnickers (*new picture,* lower centre right). Farther
back, the granite massif of Dartmoor is untameable country, the
toughest geology in the west. On the foothills and the coastal hills of
our pictures the soil is rich and the climate mild, too warm for fruit-
growing but excellent for dairy cattle, wheat, barley and vegetable
crops. But the removal of hedges and the merging of fields into
amorphous tracts for ploughing and harvesting make some parts of
the countryside, at certain times of the year, as bleak-looking as the
Moor itself. 'It's the big boys with the capital', one hears. 'The world
is their oyster now.' Not too much of a prairie oyster, one hopes.

1951

Chelmsford

'And boats adrift in yonder town go sailing up the market place' – a common occurrence when Jean Ingelow wrote her *High Tide* poem last century. Well into this century our *old picture* was a typical winter scene on the flatlands between Chelmsford and the sea. It is typical no longer.

The taming of the Chelmer river (*new picture*) has been brought about by canalizing, providing new locks, weirs and sluices and widening and banking up the bends (top centre). From bottom right, *both pictures*, the Chelmer runs six miles to the Blackwater estuary and in that distance it now has three sets of locks and two weirs and diversions. The last two miles of its route have been artificially cut to avoid Maldon's narrow corridors and conduct the river to a sea-lock opposite Northey Island.

The Chelmer (now known below Chelmsford as the Chelmer & Blackwater Canal) rises near Saffron Walden. It was never an impressive waterway, but several geographical factors enabled it to cause impressive flooding. Ages ago, along with other Essex rivers, it was a tributary of the

Thames. Then the inland swamps dried out, the land sank and the Chelmer found its own outlet to the sea. Medieval peat-cutters further lowered the land. Meantime, along England's east coast, the sea level was rising – at the rate of one foot every 100 years, it is estimated. And, since Essex sits on clay beds, surface water does not permeate very fast. Maybe the cruising craft in the Blackwater are nowadays helping to decelerate the flow: there are said to be upwards of 3000 boats afloat in the season.

Melting winter snows, coinciding with easterly winds and unusually high tides, can still produce spectacular overflows from some of the meandering Essex and Suffolk streams. Floodwaters spread over a wide region, for hills in these parts are few and are measured in tens rather than hundreds of feet.

Note, from our *two pictures*, how the fields have been enlarged and the woodlands cut back. Those centuries of inundations have built up the alluvial soil which gives the district its profitable fruit farms, market gardens, beet and cereal crops.

1956

St Mary Magdalen

If our *old picture* had been taken seven centuries ago, it would have shown nothing but water. In those days the Great Ouse seeped into swampland at Ely and entered the Wash at Wisbech. The sites of the four Wiggenhall villages – prominent here is St Mary Magdalen (*both pictures*, upper left) – were on the seabed. The Great Ouse at St Mary Magdalen is now ten miles from the Wash, nearing the end of its sluggish meandering journey across four counties. The new drain alongside the river (*new picture*) is an extension of a civil engineering programme put into effect in 1821.

But the work of Fenland reclamation and flood control, of straightening out the Great Ouse and cutting off corners to accelerate the flow, has gone on for much longer. King Charles I hired the canals expert Vermuyden to 'recover a continent of 400,000 acres' from

the Fen country in 1638. Oliver Cromwell (himself a Fenman) continued the work. Vermuyden bypassed most of the tideway from Earith with broad drains, a short-term solution which brought long-term problems. As the peat soil dried out it shrank, canal banks gave way, a wet winter put back the clock and many square miles were once again under water. Rivers and drains now flow a little above the level of the fields (*new*

picture). Hence the Fenland windmills – 700 of them at one period, pumping water uphill.

Nowadays the waterways have huge electric pumps. At Wiggenhall St Germans (*new picture*, top right) the pump discharges six million gallons a day; and during the floods which followed the heavy snows of 1947 it worked 28 days non-stop.

Hereward the Wake would think it witchcraft to see the rich farmland, the bulb

fields, the corn acres and fruit orchards which have sprung from his dismal morass. River management is costly, but it pays great dividends and there is always a chance of a bonus: here, in what was then the Wash, King John lost his jewels. Some day a mechanical digger may turn up a royal treasure hoard.

1953

Jaywick Sands

The scene is a seven-mile stretch of the Essex coast, just west of Clacton-on-Sea. In our *old picture*, Jaywick village looks forlorn, as though abandoned for good. At least the golf course (bottom right) has escaped inundation. And the Martello Tower, the round fort at the sea's edge (upper centre) sits unconcerned. It is not the first time in its two-hundred-year history that it has been islanded in muddy water.

Frequent flooding has not deterred people from making their homes, temporary or permanent, at Jaywick Sands (*new picture*).

Residents old and new have filled in every spare building plot and spread themselves along the Sands, crowding as closely as possible to the beach. From the air it suggests a neatly-planned suburb – but from the air even caravan parks (upper centre) look good. On the ground, Jaywick Sands is environmentally depressing. The original village (*new picture*, foreground and right) must not only fight the caprices of wind, rain and high tides but also resist the encroachment of unkempt, anarchic shacks and chalets, flimsy weekend cabins of

plywood and hardboard with garish paintwork or no paintwork at all. Clacton-on-Sea (bottom right, out of picture) may not be the most elegant of seaside resorts but compared with the shanty-town which runs wild along the shore it seems positively refined.

The salt marshes along this part of the Essex coast are not much use for agriculture. Cheap land, soft sands and reasonable access from London (about 90 minutes by road) have enlarged Jaywick's population by several thousand vacationists who come and go and have no real interest in the place as a community. Litter and drainage problems are a constant headache for the local authority (it may be a sewage-pipe leak that the dredger is working on in *new picture*, left). Old-time residents stand aloof. They have been heard to express the hope that another little flood will come along, not to cause loss of life but to sluice the place down. It can happen. At Jaywick sea-walls do not help because tides creep along the western creeks (to right) and take the settlement in the rear.

1953

Canvey Island

Our *old picture* records the aftermath of the floods of 1953. The Thames-side sea-walls (bottom left, not in picture) have been breached. The wall on the Benfleet side, instead of keeping the creek water out, is holding the Thames water in. The cottages and bungalows, up to their ground floors in malodorous estuary mud, preserve their smug air. They have been luckier than some on Canvey Island.

The static chalets and holiday homes of present-day Canvey (*new picture*) are enjoying better weather. For them, the possibility of disaster is remote. The sea-wall on the creek (bottom right to top left) is now a solid embankment, scientifically graded, higher than in 1953 and part of a system of protective dikes which encloses all the inhabited parts of the island.

Freak tides, accelerated by two days of tempestuous easterly gales, struck Britain's North Sea coasts early in February of that year, 1953. They washed over hundreds of square miles of Lincolnshire, Norfolk, Suffolk and Essex, lifting big ships out of dry dock at Immingham, setting small boats on aimless voyages far inland from the Crouch and Blackwater rivers, marooning vehicles on main roads even in Cambridgeshire and flooding houses and shops in many low-lying towns.

Places like Canvey Island at the mouth of the Thames were among the storm's most vulnerable targets: 58 residents were drowned that weekend. Canvey is hardly an island: only a narrow cut between two creeks makes it so. Part is a few feet below, part a few feet above sea level. For centuries it was a dangerous marsh country, water-logged and uninhabitable. Then, 350 years ago, the reclamation specialist arrived – inevitably a Dutchman – to build the first sea-wall, turn all 15 square miles into grazing ground ... and demand a third of it for himself and his relations. There are still Dutch names on tombstones round the parish church, and on the landward side (beyond left edge of *both pictures*), among abandoned timber cottages, there is a Dutch Village Museum.

Houses and people eventually replaced cattle and sheep. On the old Dutch sea-wall successive sea-walls arose, each higher than its predecessor. Victorian Canvey had a population of 300, mostly farm workers; today it has 30,000, mostly commuters, plus many weekend vacationists. Since the electrification of the London-Southend railway, more Londoners have found Canvey a convenient home or weekend resort.

Petro-chemical plants and oil refineries (Thameshaven, Shellhaven) adjoin the island, which has recently been described as 'a mixture of seaside resort, frontier town and unexploded bomb, with the additional chance of being drowned'.

It is quite a stiff climb nowadays up the embankments to look at the Thames – which, in these parts, is not much to look at. The regimented rows of temporary homes (*new picture*) seem to be elbowing the typical little cottages off the island; but overall there is a more residential, here-to-stay air about Canvey than there has been in the whole of its history.

1932

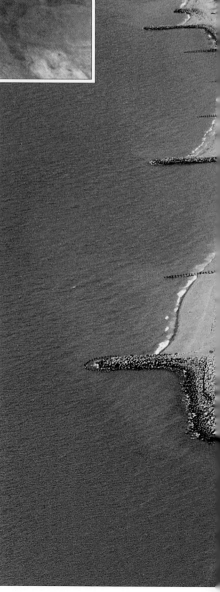

Barton-on-Sea

Towards this modern residential township of the Hampshire coast the sea has made considerable inroads. Compare the position of the golf clubhouse relative to the cliff (*old picture*, upper centre; *new picture*, centre left). The car park, adequate for the saloon cars in which a handful of members turned up during the early 1930s, is today perched on the edge of a hundred-foot drop. Erosion is inexorable. Another few years and cracks will appear in the tarmac. Some holes on the golf course have had to be shortened, others resited. Even so, a reckless chip to the green can land in the sea. Above the path to the beach (*new picture*, top left) some older buildings are at risk. Within the lifetime of some of us they will have to be vacated and will collapse.

Land masses are always on the move. Here the sea takes a bit, there it gives a bit back. On the whole, England grows bigger. Parts of the south coast have perceptibly advanced. Four Cinque Ports, for example, are now several miles inland. But other parts, like the bays of Hampshire, are scoured by the sweep of Channel currents which, through what is called 'longshore drift', displace masses of shingle and pile them up to form promontories like Chesil Beach. Brickwork, masonry and timber from Barton's golf clubhouse will probably end up one day on the pebble spit of Hurst Castle at the entrance to the Solent, five miles from the bottom of our pictures.

Barton has expanded inland, away from the threatened ribbon of turf where a cliff path (*old picture*, upper left to bottom left) has already disappeared. A little villa at Barton or Milford-on-Sea next door (two miles from bottom of the *new picture*) was long the dream of northerners contemplating retirement, for this coast was renowned for its mild climate and (the estate agent's guarantee of perfect health) its gravel soil. Half an acre of land and a few trees to go with it are no longer on offer: people live close to their neighbours. But woodland is preserved and a pleasant little glade among the built-up sections is made by the stream which trickles out across the golf course (*new picture*, lower right) to a typical Hampshire chine or 'bunny'.

1963

Loch Turret

Man-made lakes brighten and beautify landscapes just as successfully as natural ones, especially in the Highlands of Scotland, where they bring life to the desolation of rolling heather-clad hills. The dam in Glen Turret, under construction in the *old picture* (bottom right), had by 1967 trebled the length of the loch and multiplied its volume several times. After the Hydro-electric (Scotland) Act of 1943 a number of such 'finger lakes' as geologists call them – offshoots of old glaciers – became power

sources. Steep-sided hills and copious rainfall swiftly increased their capacities.

Loch Turret, however, is a reservoir. It serves the districts west of Perth and is one of Scotland's secret lochs, a broad ribbon of water two miles long in the Crieff-Lochearnhead-Aberfeldy triangle. Scarcely one public road penetrates this region. The moorland is the territory of sheep, grouse and amazingly prolific mountain hares, big as young roe-deer when fluffed out in their blue-grey winter coats. One tiny croft only (*old*

picture, centre left) was sacrificed to the loch's expansion.

Hill-walkers in summer make their way up the lochside paths, heading for the Turret Burn (*old picture*, upper centre) which leads them to the 3048-foot summit of Ben Chonzie (*old picture*, top left), the region's highest hill.

Access to this area of true solitude is not easy, but in 1987 it was permissible to drive along the private road to the dam, six miles from a main road near Crieff; though motorists were frowned on in the grouse and deer-stalking seasons.

If few tourists have seen Glen Turret, many are familiar with the Glenturret distillery at the valley foot. It claims to be Scotland's oldest, but its star attraction for visitors was Towser the distillery cat, who had slaughtered 23,029 rats and mice by her 21st birthday. Towser, a sleepy tortoiseshell, died in 1987 aged 24; but she lives on in the *Guinness Book of Records*.

1926

<u>York</u>

Some cities, and York is one, are so firmly
rooted in history that, however they might
have changed, the old always transcends the
new. When changes are made sensitively, as
in York, they only emphasize and reinforce
the ancient spirit of place. That disc of turf,
for example (*both pictures*, lower centre)
speaks as eloquently of feudal might as the
Conqueror's fortress which once stood on it.
Innocent lawns and daffodils encircling
Clifford's Tower (centre left) throw that
formidable stronghold into more vivid relief.

York is a small city (about 100,000 people)
which never spread far beyond its medieval
bounds. Yet it was the northern capital of
Rome, of the Vikings and of the English
church. And it has the longest railway
platforms in Britain.

A web of narrow lanes with cobbles,
bottle-glass windows and overhanging gables
(and some very strange names, like Whip-
ma-Whop-ma), now an all-pedestrian
'museum quarter', runs above and left of the
covered market (*old picture*, top centre) to

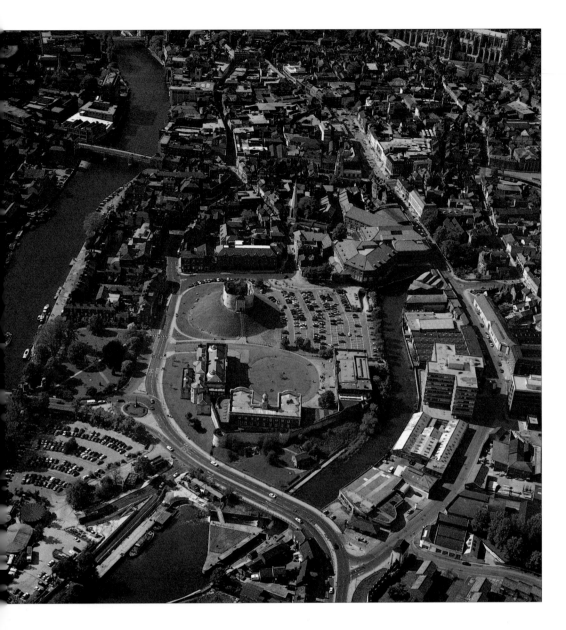

York Minster (out of picture) with its half-acre of stained glass. The medieval citadel (*both pictures*, centre) was a raised mound in the angle where Ouse and Foss rivers joined.

A women's prison, notorious in its day, beside Clifford's Tower (*old picture*) was closed in 1935. The fan-shaped cell-blocks made way for a car-park (*new picture*) and the former administrative block is now the Castle Museum.

The spire beyond the citadel (centre background) is of St Mary's church. Here and among the red-roofed buildings round it (*new picture*) is the labyrinthine heritage centre called 'York Story'. Behind the church, under Coppergate, the Viking metropolis of Yorvik has been recreated with realistic scenes, sounds and smells. Along the Ouse (top left) are the Yorkshire Museum and the National Railway Museum. The pale stone city walls are virtually intact, but the inner defensive wall (*old picture*) has been removed to open the citadel to traffic.

1924

Peterborough

Around 1970, rail passengers on the London-Edinburgh line saw the complex geometry of a 'new town' replacing the old civic heart of Peterborough. The cathedral (*new picture*, extreme right), the 17th century Guildhall and medieval parish church (both centre) remained intact. The rest of the city centre was one great building yard, controlled from Development Corporation headquarters (upper centre right). Bourges Boulevard (bottom, left to right) – Bourges is the French twin city – eased traffic congestion and created space for central all-pedestrian shopping areas and office blocks with flowery 'office parks' including Thomas Cook's world headquarters. South of the new Town Hall

(lower right) there appeared theatres, an athletics stadium and a swimming pool.

Peterborough was once a monastery in a swamp, then a cathedral village, then a 'company settlement' of 226 railway workers. As fenland agriculture improved it became a market centre for cattle, vegetables and cattle-food crops. In 1920 the first sugar-beet processing factory launched a major East Anglian industry (the British Sugar Corporation now has its head office here). Perkins' farm machinery became Perkins Diesels: the firm is now part of Massey-Ferguson, the principal local employer.

Local industries – clothing, newsprint, steam baking, brickyards of Fletton and

Brotherhood's explosives – expanded with a growing population and, after 1945, some new light industries – such as Lesney matchbox toys – arrived. But until the 'new town' upheaval of the 1970s Peterborough looked much like our *old picture* a country place with country shops and sunblinds (upper centre right), banks and cafés, Boots and Woolworths, increasingly shaken by traffic for which the streets and buildings were never designed.

'New' Peterborough has now spread over six villages and five industrial estates. With a population of 140,000 it is already close to its planned capacity.

1920

Preston

In certain lights during Wakes Week, when the factories were shut down, Preston looked like a city of 100 churches. When the workers returned, the spires became mill chimneys, pouring out smoke (*old picture* top). Today it is the new tower blocks of council housing (*new picture* centre), not the mill chimneys, which give Preston its vertical dimension. They also give the town air – clean air, because Lancashire's smoky conurbations have gone smokeless. Much else has changed, but the cherished features of a northern urban nucleus – Town Hall, Guild Hall, Library, Art Gallery and Museum and vast covered market (*both pictures* top centre) – have stood their ground.

Cynics say the new tower blocks have the effect of taking mean terraces and simply standing them on end. The workers' houses which they replaced (*old picture* foreground) look grim enough, back to back, poky and soot-encrusted in terraces devoid of greenery; but they were not quite slums, and not all crowded up against the mills of the industrial quarter (top).

The town developed as river port, railway junction and cotton centre. Horrocks, a historic textiles name, built his mill here. Arkwright and Kay perfected cotton-spinning inventions in a house which is now the town's heritage centre. The earliest cotton mills (wooden floors and low beams) remain, mostly serving other purposes. Tulketh Mill houses a mail-order firm. Cliff Mill is the Asda Superstore. Preston's population has declined, engineering is the dominant industry, cotton keeps only a third of the former workers occupied. But the town retains its old pride as a member of the élite in textiles manufacture: it specializes in weaving rather than spinning, and weaving was traditionally the more prestigious trade.

Croydon

Croydon's 330,000 inhabitants must be torn between regret for a proud community with a venerable history (*old picture*) and admiration for their modern town's daring architecture, its surrealist skyline and the soaring curve of the Croydon Flyover (*new picture* centre left) which carries traffic from the Brighton road into the heart of town. Going up Park Lane and Wellesley Road (*new picture* upper centre to upper left) you might be forgiven for imagining you were threading the skyscraper canyons of downtown Chicago.

A Town Hall like a mini St Paul's (*old picture* lower centre) and the tombs of six Archbishops of Canterbury and their former palace (bottom left) were the notable sights of old Croydon, a residential town. Landmarks for pilots approaching touch-down at Croydon airport – in the 1930s the most advanced airport in the world – were the ever-memorable 'three chimneys' (*old picture* top right). Wartime bombing provided space for urban expansion and a post-war

1937

population explosion supplied the need for it. Outside London, this is now the largest city in the south of England, and it has the densest concentration of office building in the whole of Britain.

On the left of Wellesley Road (upper left in the *new picture*) is the Whitgift Centre, a £1 million ultra-modern shopping precinct. On the right lower down (upper centre) are the elegant Fairfield Halls (1962), incorporating Concert Hall, Ashcroft Theatre and Arnhem Art Gallery. In that startling array of tower blocks is the most controversial of the 1970s buildings: Richard Seifert's N.L.A. (Noble Lowndes Annuities) House, like a 23-storey pagoda on to which a heavy weight has been dropped. Representing the architectural style of a bygone age are the Whitgift Almshouses, nestling in the concrete forest at the corner of North End and George Street (left centre in the *old picture*, hardly discernible in the *new*).

Croydon airport? It was replaced as London's airport by Heathrow in 1959 and has since been built over.

1921

Charing Cross

Waterloo Bridge (on right) was already subsiding when our *old picture* was taken. Hungerford Bridge still flaunts its utilitarian ugliness. In 1944 the present Waterloo Bridge (*new picture*) was opened. Some of the distinctive gaslamps dating from 1817 have been retained. Traffic in the *old picture* is evenly divided between horse-drawn and motorized vehicles; London's last tram ran in July 1952. In the *new picture* note the buses and tourist coaches ensnared in the Tenison Way roundabout at the south end of Waterloo Bridge. Since 1948 this south bank of the Thames has seen Britain's most astonishing cultural transformation.

It started in 1951 with the Festival of Britain on what was then a bombed and derelict site (lower centre to right).

(Remember the Dome of Discovery and the Skylon, the elliptical metal column balanced on its point? – like post-war Britain, they said: no visible means of support.) The principal South Bank halls, to the right of Hungerford Bridge in the *new picture* are the Royal Festival Hall, opened prematurely in 1951 and properly in 1965; beside it the Queen Elizabeth Hall and Purcell Room, opened 1967; and behind it the architecturally-startling Hayward Gallery, a prestigious art exhibition centre which opened in 1968 with a show of Matisse paintings.

Under Waterloo Bridge is the National Film Theatre, opened in 1957. It incorporates 'MOMI' (Museum of Moving Images, red stripes either side of the bridge in the *new picture*). On the right of Waterloo Bridge is

the new National Theatre with its large Olivier auditorium and two smaller ones, the Lyttelton and the Cottesloe. All these concert halls and theatres can accommodate a total of 8000 people.

Commerce, industry and the media have also moved into our scene. Extreme lower left in the *new picture* is part of the Shell Centre, at 400 feet the first high-rise building in London (1962). Extreme right, east of the National Theatre and the 'displaced stack' of the IBM floors, the London Weekend Television tower block can be partially seen.

Landmarks of the 'Heart of Empire', as it was in our *old picture* are landmarks still on the north bank (*both pictures*, upper centre). From left to right along the Embankment they include the Renaissance pinnacles of

Whitehall Court, left of Hungerford Bridge; Cleopatra's Needle, halfway between the bridges; and the Savoy Hotel to the left of Waterloo Bridge. Thrusting higher into the sky than anything on either bank is the 622 foot Telecom Tower (*new picture*, upper right), most dramatic element in the post-1945 London skyline.

The moored lighters in the river are gone: it is nearly all container loading now. The old-fashioned river steamers at Charing Cross Pier under Hungerford Bridge have been pensioned off, except for a few which survive as floating pubs or wine bars – such as the former Clyde paddle-steamer *Tattersall Castle* (*new picture* extreme left).

1921

Southwark

Pedestrians and lumbering commercial vehicles clutter Southwark's streets in our *old picture*, as barges and lighters clutter the Thames. Traffic on land and water moves more smoothly now. Cold stores and bonded warehouses with their nostalgic signs (*old picture*, right) took up every inch of wharf space. The new blocks are spacious and airy by comparison and you can walk to the river's edge in places and look across to Fishmongers Hall (*new picture*, bottom right). Bomb sites on Park Street (upper right) still await the developer. Riverbank buildings look a little lower than before, because each new London Bridge is higher than its predecessor; also cleaner in design and stronger (compare piers in *both pictures*).

The latest bridge (opened 1973) succeeds the bridge which now adorns a desert in America, and farther back a series of bridges of song and story, of 20 dangerous arches loaded with rickety medieval tenements, of timber structures of Saxon times and of the original Roman pontoon which first connected London camp with the market town of Southwark on the south bank. Until the middle of the 18th century, all London was served by this single bridge. (Now the Thames has 22.) London Bridge is more than a historic link. Traditionally it marks the divide between East End and West End.

In panoramic views of past and present, it is often the church which stands inviolate, mediating between conflicting fashions in architecture. Thus Southwark cathedral (*old picture*, upper centre; *new picture*, left of centre) stands – as it did when Chaucer's pilgrims assembled at the Tabard Inn, when Shakespeare acted at the Globe, when the bombs of World War II rained down on the waterfront.

Both inn and theatre, in Southwark Borough (right of cathedral) disappeared long ago. The literary pilgrim, having found only a couple of commemorative plaques, is consoled to learn that he can see the grave of Shakespeare's brother inside the cathedral.

1939

St Paul's Cathedral and the City

The City: 'riding on Ludgate Hill, escorted by her church towers and spires', as H.V. Morton wrote, and one sees what he meant. Ludgate Hill (*old picture*, centre foreground) *looks* like a hill, and St Paul's Cathedral, 'built for eternity', sits on its crown. That was before World War II cut down her escort of churches and left the City a smoking ruin.

Into the wasteland rushed the multi-million-pound office blocks and now, from the air, the 300-year-old cathedral (*new*

picture, centre, top of Ludgate Hill) is marooned in a tinted-glass, hermetically-sealed concrete and tubular steel forest. It would never have done for Queen Victoria. She set a limit of 80 feet on City buildings in case they obstructed her view from Buckingham Palace.

The most controversial construction is the steel web of Lloyd's of London (1986), a skyscraper turned inside out with pipes and girders exposed (*new picture*, left of top

centre), at the far end of Leadenhall Street. Most unfortunate is the Juxon building which spoils the view of St Paul's from Ludgate Hill. Most striking are the anorexic Stock Exchange and NatWest Tower (both top), the latter nearly twice the Cathedral's height at 690 feet. They are the latest, surely not the last, in the invasion by prestige head offices of banks, insurance companies, multinationals, Government departments and nationalized industries which started after 1945 when London resumed her role as world financial centre.

Keeping the sight-lines open to the basilica is no new problem. A 17th-century bishop complained of the thronging multitudes round Old St Paul's: 'young bankrupts, hardy ruffians, soothsayers ... purveyors of famous lies and rumours ... a noise like to that of Bees.' You could say that nothing has really changed.

1921

Piccadilly Circus

Open-topped buses, white-wheeled limousines and not many pedestrians (of whom a few stare up in astonishment at an aeroplane) make our *old picture* a period piece. Point-duty police control the traffic (Haymarket, top right); automatic signals were not installed until 1937. Flower girls ("Lovely sweet violets") in traditional black straw hats and shawls occupy their pitch round Eros (centre); they were moved away in 1925 because of heavier traffic. The beginnings of the 'neon hell' of advertising has broken out on the north side of the Circus (upper left from Eros) – Westminster City Council was even then pleading with Schweppes, Bovril and Guinness for some restraint, but the public loved the flashing lights. Eros is boarded up: no doubt Boat Race night is at hand, when revellers try to steal his bow and arrow. Rowdiness was not unknown in 1921. Mounted police were called in one night to clear the Criterion Bar (south side, right of triangle). All lamps are gas lamps. One house by Nash, the Prince Regent's architect, survives in Lower Regent Street (extreme right). It was demolished in 1939.

Principal *new picture* changes are the re-siting of Eros (centre), the restructuring of the County Fire Offices (green dome left of centre), the transformation of London Pavilion and Trocadero into a shop-restaurant-and-theatre complex (upper centre) and the modernization of buildings in Haymarket (top right) and Piccadilly (bottom right). The current traffic pattern is the latest of scores of expensive attempts to 'square the Circus'. Forty years before our *old picture* date it *was* a crossroads circus. Then they built Shaftesbury Avenue and made it (in the words of Alfred Gilbert, designer of Eros) a 'distorted isochromal triangle, square to nothing in its surroundings' – or, as the L.C.C. more succinctly put it, 'a beautiful mess'.

1926

Leeds

The City Station (*both pictures*, bottom),
under which the River Aire rushes through
the Dark Arches, dominates our views of
Yorkshire's largest city. Once it rivalled
Harrogate for the elegance of its Georgian
architecture, but most public buildings are
monuments to the city's rapid growth and
mercantile prosperity in Victorian times. The
glass-domed Corn Exchange, modelled on
Rome's Colosseum (*both pictures*, upper
right), is typical.

The railway station has been modernized.
Tower blocks of flats have appeared among
workaday redbrick terraced houses (*new
picture*, centre and upper left). Some people
liken them to the Quarry Hill flats near the
city bus station (*old picture*, top right, out of
sight) which the Town Council erected in
1935 in imitation of the famous workers' flats
of Vienna – an attempt at a brave new world
of low rents and sophisticated mod. cons. But
the experiment failed. Quarry Hill was

demolished in 1975.

Leeds was long renowned as a metropolis of markets, a shopper's paradise. In the covered city market (left and above from Corn Exchange, behind the Victorian facade), Mr Marks set up his penny bazaar which grew into Marks & Spencer. The market (*new picture*, upper right), enlarged and streamlined, stridently proclaims its northern character. There are *de luxe* shopping malls at the Bond Street Centre (*new picture*, centre, behind green dome of Mill Hill chapel) and the ultra-modern St John's Centre (upper centre left). Both areas are pedestrianized.

The city has spread north and east (top right) and encroached on the green parkland where captains of industry and commerce once built their stately villas. A new inner ring road (upper right to centre), comprising Britain's two shortest motorways, A58(M) and A64(M), makes a semi-circular detour round the heavily-congested heart of the city.

1935

Birmingham

Only now preparing to celebrate its centenary as a city, Birmingham grew furiously from humble beginnings: hence the pre-1945 chaos of 'Britain's second city' of which the chief landmarks were railway stations (*old picture* left, New Street; upper right, Moor Street). Aided by wartime bombing and clearance of sub-standard properties, the city centre has now blossomed as a triumph of massive urban renovation and redevelopment. In our *new picture* the eye travels up from a refurbished New Street station (bottom) to the old G.W.R. station at Snow Hill (centre). To the right of New Street the inner ring road goes up past the Bull Ring, once a huddle of tawdry gaslit booths on a slippery slope, now an immense multi-layered shopping and commercial complex, with big car-parks and pedestrian-only thoroughfares. Continuing north to Mass House Circus (lower right), the inner ring road swings round to Snow Hill and throws out link roads to north and north-east for the Aston Expressway (A38M) and the M6 motorway.

The inner ring road appears again in the *new picture* lower left, and connects with its northern arc near Snow Hill (lower left to centre) – passing *en route* the historic nucleus of Birmingham with its grandiose

Town Hall, Central Library and Art Gallery (inside the ring road's 'dog leg'); and St Philip's cathedral (green patch between New Street and Snow Hill). These former city-centre landmarks are quite hard to identify among so many late-20th-century monuments to progress, and are put in the shade by the dizzy height of the Telecom Tower (centre left).

Of the constructional transformation of central Birmingham, costing many millions of pounds and not yet finished, the official guidebook says that 'there is more of the future coming into being than there is of the past left to contemplate' – which naturally upsets some of the diehards. Dirty and disorganized, totally bewildering to the motorist trying to find a way through, pre-war 'Brum' inspired great affection in its inhabitants. Among childhood memories of the era when our *old picture* was taken are the hundreds of little cheap sweet stalls and second-hand clothes shops; and the scores of blue-and-white trams, motionless in line ahead, all apparently bound – if ever they got under way – for Villa Park. So broad and swift are the city-centre streets of the 1980s that they have recently been used for Grand Prix motor-racing.

Derby

In 68 years this county town has undergone modest changes which cumulatively add up to a significant transformation. Our *old picture* shows central Derby with its civic buildings and offices dwarfed, as so often in northern towns, by the Victorian Market Hall (centre) with an unostentatious Town Hall on its left and Market Place left again. The main street, Cornmarket, has trams, sun-blinds and shoppers (*old picture*, lower centre to Market Place); then it bends north, becomes Derwent Street and crosses the River Derwent (top centre). Near Morledge's lead works (edge of river gardens, right of bridge) stands the Shot Tower where lead bullets were manufactured. Up-river (top left) industrial Derby begins: iron foundry, silk mill, flour mill, the Derby electric light works (left of weir on river) and, just out of sight, the locomotive boiler works. Apart from being the ancestral home of Crown Derby china and Rolls Royce motor-cars, Derby was the Midland Railway's (later the London, Midland and Scottish Railway's) engineering centre.

Derby's old industries are gone. Even the railway works and Rolls Royce have had their

1921

ups and downs. The city ringroad (*new picture*, upper right to left) carries traffic from Nottingham to the Potteries clear of the centre. There are suburban terraces on the old factory sites; trees and green areas along the river bank (upper left). The Derwent, a shallow stream with several weirs, is altogether more attractive than it used to be. On Market Place the genteel Assembly Rooms (left of green-topped Market Hall) have been joined by a multi-storey car park.

On the sites of the defunct lead works and Shot Tower, near the river bank beside Exeter Bridge (upper centre right), are the barrack-like Council Offices. Across the river the haggard old Derwent Iron Foundry has become a large circular car park (upper right) with subway access to the ring road. Those three-and four-storey buildings in St James's and Victoria Streets (*old picture*, left foreground) were hotels and banks in 1921. Now they are bigger banks and government offices. In an English county town the administration demands ever more space, and prime space too.

1969

Gravelly Hill

Few people outside Birmingham have heard of Gravelly Hill, but Spaghetti Junction is a household expression. They are one and the same place. In *both pictures* centre, the two focal points of Aston reservoir, a canal feeder (by the gravel pits), and Salford athletics stadium are prominent. Suburban housing towards Erdington (top right) has escaped drastic change and acquired some leafy landscaped greenery. The rest is almost unrecognizable under this astonishing nexus of grand routes from all parts of England and the engineering and electronics factories it has called into existence – factories in no way dependent on the traditional Black Country iron-based industries. In that district, beyond top and left of *both pictures* only one blast furnace survives and the old trades of nail, hammer, bolt, lock, girder and chain-cable manufacture have been virtually wiped out.

Before the motorways came, Gravelly Hill was a Spaghetti Junction of canals. From the south (*old picture* bottom and right) arrived the Worcester & Birmingham and the Stratford canals. To the north (top and left) went the Rushall and the Birmingham & Fazeley canals. They had links nationwide, via the Grand Union, the Shropshire Union, the Trent & Mersey canals and the River Severn. Birmingham, it was said, had more canal mileage than Venice.

To build the motorway interchanges it was necessary to clear housing and divert a river and a canal. Opened on 24th May 1972, this most complicated of traffic junctions merges 18 separate routes on six separate levels. It needed 250,000 tons of concrete – the crushed gravel came, not from Gravelly Hill, but from the Rowley Regis quarries in the Black Country.

The principal routes seen in the *new picture* are the M6 northbound (top left), the M6 southbound (lower right) and the Aston Expressway (A38M) into central Birmingham (lower left). The tangle of sliproads and flyovers is striking in an aerial view, but to appreciate the grandeur and complexity of the work you must go underneath, along the towpath of an old chocolate-coloured canal, where forests of Cyclopean concrete pillars support the criss-crossing undersides of the carriageways.

1946

Poplar and Bromley-by-Bow

This is the Cockney heartland. Before traffic
noises shut out the sound, you could hear
Bow Bells. You found a polyglot population
too: residents of Huguenot, Irish, Jewish and
Italian refugee descent along with seafarers of
all the nations, for great dock systems
flourished in Poplar (West and East India
Docks) and Millwall (Millwall Docks) next
door. The area was persistently targeted by
enemy bombers in the Second World War.
After the first heavy raid of 7th September
1940, Bromley and Poplar suffered 76
consecutive nights of air-raids and 100 more
over the next few months.

Ground thus ruthlessly cleared (*old picture*)
enabled local councils to create gardens and
ensure that no future citizen would boast, as
slum dwellers had done, of living and dying
without knowing what green grass looked
like. Symbolic of the clean sweep was the
name (actually an old medieval name) of
Tower Hamlets, embracing Poplar, Stepney
and Bethnal Green. 'Tower' was apt: they had
some of London's biggest and most
imaginative high-rise flats. (But the collapse

of Ronan Point in a gas explosion in 1968
made East End authorities think again about
the wisdom of marooning council tenants in
low-cost tower blocks hundreds of feet above
terra firma.)

In the *new picture* two gas-tanks survive
(centre left background) along with clumps of
pre-war housing marked for demolition. The
whole area has been opened out and given
space to breathe. Trees and shrubs are
reaching maturity. Poplar's fine neo-classical
parish church, All Saints (East India Dock
Road, lower right), came through the war
unscathed.

The population is still mixed, with many
post-war immigrants from India and
Pakistan. Diehard natives are apprehensive
about the London Docks Development
Council's scheme for bringing in costly
offices and luxury flats for high-salaried City
executives, all under the banner of urban
regeneration. Already Poplar has one high-
tech marvel, the new Billingsgate Fish
Market on the docks.

1932

Manchester

Our *old picture* evokes the town-planner's nightmare: classic mid-Victorian back-to-backs on monotonous streets, 'built by the mile and cut off by the yard', fated to degenerate into slums, too poky ever to be upgraded yet too solidly built to be bulldozed away. They were, however, eventually cleared and Moss Side's population of 65,000 came down to 30,000. The dramatic drop occurred when large-scale redevelopment got under way between 1971 and 1981.

Bottom (*both pictures*) is Alexandra Park, now furnished with recreation grounds and play areas. Upper centre (*new picture*) is the Moss Side Shopping and Leisure Centre, to its left St Mary's church (clearly seen in the *old picture*), a listed building destined to be the focus of a multi-denominational 'worship centre'. From top to lower right runs Princess Road, widened and straightened, the route between central Manchester and its airport. It has a cycle track.

Inset shows, in a frame of green lawns, the Alexandra Park estate, a low-rise council housing project of the 1970s – no garden city, perhaps, but environmentally a world away from the hopeless squalor of a bygone era.

Manchester was the capital of cotton spinning, the Industrial Revolution's first industry. It quickly became the powerhouse of machinery and machine-tool manufacture for the Lancashire mills and factories. As 'Cottonopolis' it had the best and the worst of everything – virtues, vices, education, ignorance. 'Frequently maligned by those who never knew it, regarded with affection by those who did', as a local historian wrote, the city was synonymous with working-class political aspirations and cultural self-improvement. Karl Marx came 20 times to Manchester in 20 years. No doubt he heard the Hallé Orchestra at the Free Trade Hall, or attended some great assembly there. Maybe he met P.M. Roget (of the *Thesaurus*), who was first secretary of the handsome Portico Library.

Since our *old picture* was taken, Greater Manchester has absorbed several neighbouring towns. The city itself, for long years a seemingly uncontrollable, densely-crowded sprawl, has since 1945 shrunk to a more manageable size.

Gorbals

Bird's eye views can be misleading. Our *old picture* shows a stately city gathered on the banks of the majestic Clyde. You had to alight on a Gorbals rooftop (lower centre) to appreciate the abysmal squalor in which 15,000 Glaswegians were submerged. Touring the Gorbals today (*new picture*, lower left and centre), visitors ask: "When are we coming to the Gorbals?" The grim four-and five-storey tenements characteristic of Scottish cities were all cleared away in the 1950s and the inhabitants transferred to the new tower blocks, and to suburban housing estates and overspill towns. There are still ugly holes in the ground (*new picture*, bottom right); cindery wastes which no one seems to know what to do with; and graffiti-covered walls. But those who live and work in the Gorbals today have vistas of a Victorian townscape which they never knew they possessed. Their exit to the heart of Glasgow is via riverbank shrubbery on a cleaned-up Clyde devoid of seagoing ships. The foot suspension bridge takes them to a flowery Clyde Walkway (*new picture*, centre right) where the historic clipper-ship *Carrick* (R.N.V.R. headquarters, lower right) has come to rest.

They were chiefly destitute Highland and Irish families, coming to the big city in search of a better life which they did not find, who first populated the Gorbals. (That broad low railway bridge out of Central station, centre of *old picture* was contemptuously known as the 'Hielandman's Umbrella'.) In the 1930s the quarter was notorious for a moral and physical ugliness unsurpassed in Europe and was the object of many a social survey and many an inconclusive official enquiry. Novelists and playwrights took ghoulish pride in exposing the misery and degradation of the Gorbals.

In retrospect it is easier to paint the vivid horrors of slum life than to portray its consolations. In the clearances of the 1950s many tenement-dwellers fought stubbornly to stay in the Gorbals, and wept when forced to leave their homes.

1936

1933

Cardiff

Our views look westward, across the River Taff (*old picture*, upper left) towards Llandaff and the Vale of Glamorgan. The main road to west Wales is now pedestrianized and tree-lined in the town centre (*new picture*, lower centre) and the traffic system takes motorists on a circular tour (bottom to centre right). Focused on the pedestrian-only avenue is Cardiff's main shopping precinct, criss-crossed with arcades. On the sites of war-damaged and decayed housing, a few high-rise flats and office blocks have arisen (*new picture*, bottom left) along streets named for Prince Charles and Winston Churchill. There

is room for more on vacant lots. By contrast, Llandaff across the river is still the same old jumble of lowly terraces, with embryo industrial estates beyond them.

Cardiff Arms Park, the international rugby ground (*both pictures*, upper left on river bank) shows only superficial changes but in reality has been expensively updated. Nearby (*new picture*, extreme left) is the jewel in Cardiff's athletics crown, the Wales Empire Pool.

Shabbiest of European capitals, with the possible exception of Dublin, the city is improving its looks step by step. The best

architecture is out of our *pictures*: the older marine buildings of dockland (left of bottom left) and the classical civic centre which gleams in Portland stone (right of top right). Outclassed by their dignity and out-topped by the skyscrapers, one of which has 23 storeys, are the landmarks of Cardiff's historic heart: the Norman fort (*old picture*, upper right) and Cardiff Castle, a Victorian extravaganza, beside it. They stand like the twin guardians of Bute Park (upper right), resisting the advance of new roads to which woodland (lower right) has already been sacrificed.

Coventry

Coventry was a city of three spires – two of them, St Michael's cathedral and Holy Trinity (centre right and centre left) are visible in the *old picture*. There was also a fine 14th-century Guildhall (opposite cathedral) and a large covered market (lower left); and numerous ancient hospitals and almshouses. The town of Leofric and Godiva and of harsh confinement in the Civil War (hence 'sent to Coventry') kept its medieval and Elizabethan quarter intact (*old picture*, lower centre) long after the transport era brought industry to its gates and submerged its outskirts first under bicycles (Rudge-Whitworth and others), then motor-cycles (Triumph and others) and then cars (Rover, Daimler, Wolseley and 60 other makes).

Much of historic Coventry was swept away on 14th September 1940 when one of the heaviest air raids experienced in Britain destroyed its centre (*wartime picture*). The city immediately became the 'down-but-not-out' prototype. Rebuilding was a national priority, an act of faith in the future. 'Rain comes in but shops are well-stocked and housewives smile' was the *Illustrated London News* 1949 caption to pictures of the blitzed market arcade.

Amazingly, the distinctive spires (*new picture*, centre) survived. From the rubble of the cathedral a new and controversial building arose. The City Council rejected the plan as 'too modern' but was overruled by the Government. Graham Sutherland's high altar tapestry, John Piper's baptistery window and Epstein's *St Michael and the Devil* attracted both praise and condemnation.

Completed in 1962, the cathedral is now a major tourist attraction. By that date a science-fiction city had risen around it, locked in an elevated ring-road (*new picture*, foreground and upper centre). Some of Britain's best looking high-rise offices and apartment blocks sprang up. Outward and upward the city continued its rapid growth for a decade, until hit by recession and rationalization of the motor industry.

1920

1946

1938

Letchworth

Ebenezer Howard's little books *Tomorrow: A Peaceful Path to Real Reform* and *Garden Cities of Tomorrow* did not reach the bestseller lists. With titles like that, they could hardly be expected to. But they had an impact on town and country planning beyond their author's most extravagant expectations. They inspired the foundation of the Garden City Association (1899).

Four years later the Association formed a company, First Garden City Ltd, and bought 4,000 acres of land near the Hertfordshire village of Letchworth, on the Hitchin-Cambridge railway. The line and the minor roads which ran parallel with it formed the framework of the Garden City layout: the *old picture* indicates how a rectilinear street pattern was imposed on existing lanes and pathways.

In that picture, top, tree-lined Norton Way crosses the railway en route to an area of unspoiled parkland. Centre of the *old picture* is the embryo Town Square (the *new picture* shows the eventual fountain, rosebeds and screen of poplars). The main approach road, Broadway (*both pictures*, bottom right), is an avenue of lime trees. Town centre buildings (*new picture*, upper and lower centre) include the Town Hall (1935), the Museum and Art

Gallery (1914, enlarged 1962) and the bandstand-like Roman Catholic church of St Hugh (1962).

Letchworth's houses, built under lease from First Garden City Ltd, were the prestige redbrick suburban 'villas', with good gardens conferring privacy and a sycamore tree for everyone, that so many 1930s owner-occupiers aspired to. The industrial estate, a feature previously unheard of, was at the other end of town near the railway. Businesses were slow to move in, and F.G.C. Ltd was choosy about whom it accepted. The large office blocks (top left) appeared only in the late 1960s. The main shopping area, behind the Town Square, is noted for its good design and ample parking space.

Letchworth's growth has been steady rather than spectacular: 12,000 in 1925, 32,000 now. It was the pioneer of garden cities, ante-dating the more celebrated Welwyn Garden City (see pages 96-97), a few miles south by 17 years. Property speculators engineered a takeover in 1960, but clamour from residents brought about an Act of Parliament and a Letchworth Corporation to protect the community and maintain Ebenezer Howard's ideals.

1939

1928

Welwyn Garden City

Both pictures, *old* and *new* span the 60-year growth of Britain's second Garden City. Founded in 1920 on 1,688 acres of Hertfordshire countryside, Welwyn by the date of our *old picture* had achieved the rectilinear plan of tree-lined avenues which would form the street network of the town centre; and it had a railway station on the main L.N.E.R. line (top left).

Eleven years later (*interim photograph*) the town had a population of 10,000 and the public buildings were complete. With its formal gardens, fountains, boulevards and radial curves, Welwyn looked distinctly Frenchified – which was not surprising because its architect was Louis de Soissons. Rows of houses conformed to the geometrical pattern, but individually they displayed a mixture of styles, with what has been called a 'comfortable neo-Georgian' predominating. They were built at ten to the acre, a very low density at the time. They had sizeable back

gardens and strips of lawn in front. Shrubs and flowering trees were healthy and prolific. The well-wooded hill slopes to the north (we are looking south) had not been disturbed.

Welwyn Garden City was declared a 'new town' in 1948. In the *new picture* it has reached a near-maximum population of 41,000 – and has several mature trees to every inhabitant. The pioneers' enthusiasm has made Welwyn more of a Forest City than a Garden City.

Unlike its precursor and neighbour, Letchworth (see pages 94-95), Welwyn is acclaimed as a fine example of social engineering and a delightful and interesting place to visit. The public buildings have spread themselves with the proliferation of local government departments. Important residential and light-industrial developments have urbanised the east side of the railway (upper left). But a variegated architecture offers attractive vistas and cameos as you tour

the avenues; and the immediate neighbourhood is still leafy and haunted with wildlife, including deer. The 'green belt' separating Welwyn from Hatfield (top right) has only sports grounds on it.

Garden City philosophy demanded a smooth mix of social classes: no palaces, no ghettoes. But human nature has made the railway line a deep divide – middle classes to the right, the proletariat to the left.

1921

Epsom

There is an explanation for what in 1921 (*old picture*) is heavy motor traffic. Tomorrow is Derby Day, when half a million people on the Downs will see Steve Donoghue ride *Humorist* to victory – the first of that jockey's three successive Derby winners.

Originally built near a curative spring, Epsom was an exceptionally pretty town. It has grown enormously (compare top left beyond the railway in *both pictures*), but not ungracefully. The railway station (*new picture* upper left) is greatly enlarged and modernized; in the old days you could cross the line only by a public road under it (*old picture* upper right centre). Motorists parked more or less indiscriminately round the clock tower in the market place (*old picture* centre). Nowadays a market centre of affluent Surrey needs abundant parking space – and Epsom has it (*new picture* upper left near railway; upper right behind shops; centre; and centre left, a multi-storey car park). Low-rise flats, offices and supermarkets in a relatively spacious setting (*new picture* centre and right) occupy the land between the roads to Banstead and the Downs, formerly an enclave of little gabled Victorian houses and smallholdings which diffused scents of the country over the heart of the town.

Major housing developments have taken place north of the Banstead road (centre right) and all the way to Ewell (top right, between branching railways). Round the gasworks (top right) was a colony of

dull terraces, most of which have been cleared. Epsom's exit to the
north-east is lined with modern four-storeyed terraces in pleasing neo-
Georgian style, with extensions to the main-street shopping area
underneath and parking space at the back (*new picture* upper right).
They replace a tangle of old properties, picturesque but insanitary (*old
picture* centre right), on a dreaded bottleneck of a street. This was the
main London road: the most rapid expansion of the town which, with
Ewell, now has 70,000 inhabitants, has been in this direction.

You still detect a touch of Regency flair on Epsom's broad market
place. It was once a thoroughfare for the slower stage-coaches from
London to Brighton – those whose passengers preferred the prettier
route, and were not averse to a prolonged halt at the Tangier Inn on
the Downs, to sample its renowned elderberry wine. Through traffic
now goes along the A217 dual carriageway to the east (extreme right,
out of pictures). The racecourse is two miles beyond the park and
southern suburbs (*new picture* foreground).

Epsom's racing traditions go back to the Elizabethans, who found
the green turf of the chalk downs ideal for training and exercising
horses. The Derby and The Oaks (the name of Lord Derby's house
near Epsom) were inaugurated 200 years ago. The curative waters
('Epsom salts') spring from a covered well at a school (top right near
railway, out of pictures)

Scunthorpe

Old picture: the forecast says acid rain over the Baltic. But at that period acid rain had not been invented and smoke abatement was the childish dream of idealists who understood nothing about the economics of heavy industry. Scunthorpe in Lincolnshire was then responsible for almost a quarter of Britain's iron and steel production. Its forests of smoky chimneys constituted one of the nation's major black spots. In the slump after the Second World War the first coke ovens and blast furnaces to go were the oldest and dirtiest, such as these along the Normanby road, just north of Frodingham. Cleaner and less obtrusive industries – electrical engineering, railway trackwork, paint manufacture, metal rod and mild steel products – occupy the levelled sites. On the Borough Council's estate taking shape in the *new picture* are the Byfleet Works, for machine tools, industrial maintenance and metal spraying. On the Trent (upper right) is Flixborough, scene of the catastrophic explosion of 1974 at Nypro Chemicals.

Iron ore, first exploited in 1860, made a steel town of the poor village of Scunthorpe. Output started in 1890, after which growth in production and population and the ravaging of the countryside with quarries went steadily ahead. Pig iron and steel are still very important: under renationalization in 1967, British Steel revived hopes of full employment with a 200-million pound plant and rolling mills. About one-eighth of all the nation's steel still comes from Scunthorpe, and her 'Four Queens' are among the nation's most powerful blast furnaces. But the numbers of men at work in the industry continue to decline.

Pollution controls and the switch to planned industrial estates have given the local council the confidence to proclaim Scunthorpe an 'Industrial Garden City'. Housing developments and shopping and leisure areas are cheerful and modern and there is a fine new covered market. With its own airport and motorway (M181, due to be extended across our *new picture* to the Humber Bridge), the town is certainly not as black as some have painted it.

1951

1938

St Katherine Dock

The jigsaw pattern of basins, wharves and loading berths which begins at Tower Bridge and continues to Tilbury 26 miles away, cutting across loops in the Thames, is the Port of London. Less busy than formerly, it nevertheless handles ten per cent of Britain's exports and nearly 20 per cent of her imports. As you sail down-river, the first system on the north bank is the London docks; and the first of these, in the very shadow of Tower Bridge, is St Katherine Dock, so called because it was dug (in 1828) out of the foundations of the ancient collegiate church of St Katherine-by-the-Tower.

It had a noble setting. The Royal Mint was alongside it. The Tower of London (*old picture* centre left) was just across the street. The dock, the highest up-river which ocean-going vessels could enter, dealt in exotic commodities – 'ivory, apes and peacocks, sandalwood, cedarwood and sweet white wine'. But it was the smallest of the London docks, the Cinderella of the system.

London's dockland, badly hit by air raids in the Second World War, had been designed for small sailing ships. Despite some

widening and deepening, it could not be equipped to handle huge
modern vessels or cope with technological change – containerization,
roll-on-roll-off – except far downstream at Tilbury, where an
enormous grain terminal and the world's largest refrigerated container
terminal (1978) were installed. The main London docks (*both pictures*
centre right) have been filled in and built over. The river lighters (*old
picture*) are no more. St Katherine Dock, the neglected Cinderella, is
now the fairy-tale princess. Grizzled longshoremen who knew the
river of old stand bewildered at this maritime village of shops, cafés,
flower-beds and 'museum' boats; most of all at the smart yachts and
cabin cruisers which throng the marina where rusty salt-caked tramp
steamers used to lie. The Ivory warehouse is now Ivory House, a block
of luxury flats. The castellated building beside Tower Bridge is the
826-room Tower Thistle Hotel. Behind it, running along the dock
wall, is the World Trade Centre. The whole complex is now a bright
haven for yachtsmen and tourists.

Brixham

Gracie Fields's 1930s song hit, *Red Sails in the Sunset* must have been written with Brixham in mind. This archetypal fishing port, a gem of quaintness, lies close to Torquay and Paignton and not far off the route of the Cornish Riviera express and the scenic Dart Valley line (*old picture*, viaducts top centre and right). Brixham boats had red sails. All family-owned, generally with a father-and-son crew, the fleet comprised both inshore and deep-sea craft, the larger boats being sailing trawlers or drifters with auxiliary engines. They took herring in winter – the drifters laying out miles of nets to do so – and mackerel and pilchard at other times. Pilchards were the ingredients of stargazy pie and tiddy oggy, regional delicacies which helped to establish a Devon and Cornwall cuisine.

1928

It caused sentimental anguish but it was inevitable; Brixham joined Torquay and Paignton to form the borough of Torbay, where the chief industry is not fishing but tourism. Cosy cottages once offered lodgings to landscape painters – smart hotels now encircle a port crammed with pleasure craft among which a surviving Brixham trawler would look archaic. Step ashore at the new marina (*new picture*, centre) and you step into a waterfront village of shops, repair sheds, fuel points, bars and discos. It is the same in the inner harbour (centre left).

Deep-sea fishing has declined. Fuel is expensive and the pilchard are elusive nowadays. Brixham's remaining fishermen compete with French and Spanish boats, chiefly for mackerel, which is distributed fresh, frozen or canned to faraway markets.

1925

Grimsby

To say that when the trawlers were in you could walk across the Fish Dock on their slippery decks would be to exaggerate; but not by much. The deep-sea fleet in its post-1918 heyday was numbered in hundreds. They formed long acrimonious queues to get in through the lock gates. They were big, cumbersome boats for their time, often needing tugs (*old picture*, centre right and lower centre) to manoeuvre inside the basin.

The modern diesel trawler looks no bigger but she does more work – when she can get it. The industry's decline and rationalization is exemplified (*new picture*) in the clean spare lines of modern boats, and all the vacant spaces at the jetties. Ancient mariners, remembering the jostle at the Fishmarket (*old picture*, centre right) and the cluttered sheds, treacherous with fish heads and scales, and the noisy stampedes of porters across the cobbles with herring-boxes on trolleys, must stand amazed at the serenity and good order of the new shed (*new picture*, centre), a

capacious enclosed tunnel angled to the full length of the wall. Light craft and inshore fishing boats have their moorings (lower left) in what used to be graving docks for the repair and building of trawlers (*old picture*, lower left).

Grimsby and nearby Hull, deadly seafaring rivals, were Britain's largest fishing ports. The trawlerman's stamping-ground was the bitter north: Iceland, the White Sea, the Barents Sea, the Denmark Strait. Calamity struck with the Cod Wars, when Iceland established her 200-mile-radius exclusion zone. Since then there have been international embargoes on herring fishing. Promised benefits from E.E.C. membership have not materialized and a number of trawler owners and skippers have been forced to diversify or go out of business. The action has shifted from the Fishmarket to the frozen-food, pet-food and fertilizers factories, for it is on fish fingers and the like that much of Grimsby's prosperity now depends.

Southampton

High season on the Atlantic run and at the Trafalgar Dock the four-funnelled *Aquitania* (45,500 tons) is raising steam for another dash across the 'herring pond', Southampton to New York in five days. Before her farewell voyage in 1949, this great Cunarder (*old picture* upper centre) will have completed more than 600 Atlantic crossings. Other transatlantic liners in the *old picture* are the

Homeric (centre) and the *Olympic* (lower centre) – the latter a sister-ship of the sunken *Titanic*.

The docks were a fussy, ramshackle collection of warehouses, workshops, tugs, floating cranes, dredgers and miscellaneous harbour craft, hedged in with tangles of railway sidings. Compare the new-look, open and streamlined waterfront of today (*new*

1923

picture). Freight traffic is largely containerized, loaded and discharged with push-button simplicity at the new docks which extend for nearly a mile north-west along a formerly empty shoreline (*old picture* top centre). Southampton's heliport is just behind them. Cruise liners still berth at the historic landing-stages but the almost daily bustle of boat-trains and mail vans and

baggage-porters of 60 years ago is a tale of the past.

Southampton docks were built out on a shallow promontory at the meeting of the Test and Itchen (far right, not visible) rivers, which gave them a long waterfront. The eight-mile sea channel of Southampton Water and the barrier of the Isle of Wight at the end of it provided perfect shelter. More important for the fast turn-round of shipping, there is – due to the vagaries of tidal streams – high water four times a day and consequently a small rise and fall; which means that this port, uniquely in northern Europe, needs no lock gates on her docks.

Old-timers miss the ostentatious majesty of the transatlantic liners, the leviathans which towered over cranes and church spires. (You could have run two trains side by side down each of the *Aquitania's* funnels.) Somehow the *Queen Elizabeth 2*, a heavier ship, does not dominate the scene the way her predecessors did. The harbour is more spread out and more roomy. It looks deserted (*new picture*), but plenty is going on around it. Apart from the container ships and bulk carriers, there are car ferries to Le Havre (from Royal Pier, uppermost of quays in *new picture*) and to Cowes, Isle of Wight (from Town Quay next door). Hydrofoils and hovercraft have their own terminals (extreme right, out of picture). Oil tankers more gigantic than anything Cunard or White Star ever built pass in procession up the Solent to Fawley on Southampton Water, to a petro-chemical centre from which fuel goes to Britain's power stations and aviation spirit is piped direct to London's Heathrow airport.

1946

Birkenhead

Liverpool calls it her 'ugly sister' – a case of Satan rebuking sin. Visitors do find the capital of the Wirral an uninviting place at first glance. 'What this town needs is a good bath,' a foreign architect wrote – and to some extent the peculiarly gritty blackness of a bygone age (*old picture*) has been removed. Beneath the grime, closer inspection revealed some solid Victorian terraces (*old picture* centre left); the handsome stone-fronted Hamilton Square with its cupola'd Town Hall (centre); and Sir Joseph Paxton's florid 225-acre Birkenhead Park (top), which served as a model for New York's Central Park. Although the heavy air raids of September 1940 created bare spaces in the town centre, all those features are identifiable in the *new picture*. But Birkenhead's famous tramway system (*old picture*, centre right), the first in Europe (1860), is gone. New government-aided industry, swift approaches from the Wirral motorway to the Mersey Tunnel (upper left), and car parks have only partly filled the waste ground of demolished factories and houses.

The sad changes are in the shipyards and docks (*new picture*, centre left and upper right). Shipbuilding was the principal industry, the barometer of prosperity and despair. Birkonians had no promenade on the Mersey, no beach – the whole waterfront bristled with graving docks and slipways. Cammell Laird's, one of naval shipbuilding's Big Five, produced the *Ark Royal*, the *Prince of Wales*, numerous cruisers and more recently nuclear submarines. The laying of a keel is a rare event now.

The docks (upper right) on the Birken river are also a gloomy picture. Once they rivalled Liverpool in tonnages of American wheat and West Indian sugar handled at the wharves and processed in dockside flour mills and sugar refineries. The mammoth soap factory at Port Sunlight depended on copra and palm-oil cargoes brought into Birkenhead. Nowadays the most regular arrivals at the renovated but increasingly forlorn-looking docks are the cattle boats from Ireland. Significantly, when the Mersey prepared to receive the big oil tankers, the authorities sited the terminal at Tranmere, a few miles up the river. This Wirral shore grows increasingly densely populated and industrialized, but parts of its 'capital', Birkenhead, begin to resemble a quiet oasis.

mid 1930s

Hanley

Our *old picture* was taken during holiday week: when those coal-fired bottle ovens are lit up the whole landscape is blotted out. With fewer chimneys than the Lancashire towns, Staffordshire's Potteries produced far more smoke. Hanley, pictured here, heart of the 'Five Towns', was Charles Dickens's 'Coketown'.

The greening of the Five Towns began in 1971 with the dismantling of the last bottle ovens and the planting of grass on waste ground and slag-heaps. It continued with award-winning reclamation schemes and a forest park for Hanley (*new picture* top left beyond dual carriageway). The *new picture* shows the relative brightness of the Potteries scene where once, they said, schoolchildren would use black crayons for drawing trees. Our *old picture*, not so very old, displays no motor cars; ill-paid workers in the world's greatest porcelain, china and earthenware centre lived in drab redbrick terraces (*old picture* top left) and scarcely aspired to bicycles. Blocks of old dwellings survive (*new picture* bottom centre and upper right), but demolition has given Hanley parking space and, if residents take little pride in their poky houses or cheap high-rise flats, they nearly all have a shiny motor car standing outside.

Pottery is now fired electrically in modern or renovated workshops and the monotonous jobs of applying handles, painting designs and suchlike are almost totally automated. The last bottle oven of all is now the Gladstone Pottery Museum at Longton.

Pre-1939 warehouses still hug the banks of the Caldon canal (*both pictures* left and upper centre) along which barge-loads of Cornish china clay, French flints and Argentinian bone came to the potbanks. 'Blueways' for pedestrians now follow the towpaths, matching the 'Greenways' of the Potteries' disused railway tracks. This canal is strictly for holiday craft – a voyage into industrial history of which in a few years there may be hardly a trace.

Corby

The parliamentary candidate asked his prospective constituent what was the principal industry in those parts of Northamptonshire. "Foxhunting," came the prompt reply. But within a few years the quickset hedges, copses, spinneys and grassy fields were being bulldozed into terraces of grey limestone rubble (*old picture* top left) and Stewart & Lloyds' smelters were laying down a smoke-screen (lower centre) over the Rockingham Forest.

Since the date of our *old picture* open-cast mining of iron ore and steel production at Corby have boomed and declined. After 1945 the steelworks expanded enormously (*new picture* upper left). Roads and rail sidings proliferated (lower left and upper right). But steel production ceased in 1981 and the foul smoke of the *old picture* is only a memory. Open-cast eyesores exist – mining around Corby was more like quarrying – but large areas have been levelled off (*new picture* lower left), topsoil has been replaced to a depth of 80 feet in places and some of the scarred land has been returned to agriculture. Here and

there around Weldon (*new picture* top) the classic double-oxer hedges of the hunting country are again holding up their heads.

Rockingham Forest's very name evokes a Jeffrey Farnol romance of beaux and bucks and knights of the whip. From Regency times it was known to contain iron ore. Twentieth-century technology found a way of mining it commercially but, since it was of low grade, transport to the steel manufacturing towns was prohibitive. The company therefore built a production plant on the spot. In its palmy days, the 1940s to 1960s, the village of Corby (population 1400, bottom of *pictures* out of sight) became a settlement of 15,000 and eventually a planned 'new town' of 45,000 people.

Recession finally spread into the East Midlands. At Corby a much-reduced work force makes only steel tubes. The economy has reversed itself: iron ore, once sent to Tees-side, is now brought from Tees-side. In 1987 a 'major industrial development' at Corby, involving a huge injection of public money, was proposed.

1938

mid 1930s

Halifax

They sliced the millstone grit (its very name suggests harsh stubborn toil) to make a clearing for the town. Dark satanic mills arose, commanding rail sidings and acres of squalid cottages amid shale and rock. Mill owners considered it an act of philanthropy to put the workers next door to their place of work. Icy winds swept through the gorge, carrying away some of the smoke. The pretty Calder river ran foul with industrial waste – Halifax specialized in heavy woollens, blankets, carpets and the like, the dirty unhealthy end of the trade. The view from Beacon Hill looked down on what the Victorians called the Devil's Cauldron.

In the *old picture* the back-to-back cottages are tiny replicas of the mills, prison-like, without frills. But deliverance was always at hand in the romantic canyons and bleak moorland of Calderdale and the Wuthering Heights country to the north-west. Climb any hill out of Halifax and you had not only impressive panoramas of industry but also a perspective of the Pennine ridge, perhaps the

most dramatic landscape in England before the factories came. At weekends a twopenny bus-ride or a half-hour's walk enabled you to breathe clean air on the crags and hilltops. From towns like Halifax the 1920s hiking craze sprang.

The *new picture* shows improved housing, landscaped parks and fast new roads which make short work of the valley trough and escarpment en route to the trans Pennine motorway, the M62. Mill chimneys are gone – the industry is not dead, but it no longer depends on coal, and fluctuations in world wool prices, along with competition from synthetic fibres, have seriously damaged it. A few mills are preserved for tourism.

The old escape routes to the hills are now waymarked trails on the 50-mile Calderdale Way. The city centre Piece Hall, where merchants haggled over 'pieces' (sample lengths of wool) is an exhibition centre. The guillotine dreaded by vagabonds ('From Hull, Hell and Halifax, good Lord deliver us') is displayed in the museum.

Huddersfield

J.B. Priestley called his fictional town 'Bruddersford' – a name which combined two archetypes of harsh, grubby, north-country industry, Huddersfield and his birthplace Bradford. But the *old picture* shows some rolling countryside at the gates of Huddersfield. There were stately homes and deer parks, and the town itself was the aristocrat of woollen manufacture. Its mills dealt with the light quality worsteds which went into the city slicker's suit at the multiple retailers.

Tortuously ranged over the confluence of several steep river valleys, the place stood aloof from its neighbours. It had a well-planned centre with some dignified Victorian buildings, a Town Hall which would not have looked out of place in Renaissance Italy, a pseudo-Palladian railway station (*old picture*, centre left). The Huddersfield Choral Society, with which the late Sir Malcolm Sargent made his reputation, exemplified a strong musical tradition.

Dense conglomerations of mills lined the river and canal banks (*old picture*, centre right and bottom right), soulless and grim, capable of laying down an umbrella-barrage of smoke on the valleys. Some mills were tiny, tucked away in corners, devoted to obscure trades; one or two made clogs.

The *new picture* shows how newer, cleaner factories have invaded the same areas. World recession closed many mills and, although textiles and clothing manufacture are still the mainstay, there are transport and construction companies too, and various kinds of medium and light engineering.

At today's chimneyless, roomy, automated mill you may buy fabrics, velvets and knitwear. In a completely renovated civic centre and law courts, architectural modernism has run riot with glass and sharp angles. Broad access roads speed traffic into a notoriously congested town centre. Conservationists have rescued some valleys and waterways, notably the Huddersfield Narrow canal, a seven mile route to Marsden. And on Holme Moss, only six miles from town, the paths, ravines, wildlife and stone-built hamlets of the moors begin.

1934

1936

Oldham

Here, they say, began the process which turned farming England into a factory. Eighteenth-century Oldham already had 50 cotton mills, like prisons with blank walls and tiny skylights, fortified against mob attack. It was the noisiest town in the north. 'Every rural sound is sunk in the clamour of the works,' wrote John Byng in 1790.

A prosperous place (for some), vigorously responding to world demand, it quickly swallowed adjacent villages. Its mills grew from 120 in 1866 to 240 in 1883 and 330 at the date of our *old picture*. Terraces of tough, compact workers' houses went up (foreground). Many still exist (*new picture*, lower centre). One third of the 90,000 houses in this L.S. Lowry townscape are of pre-1919 vintage.

Oldham's cotton industry achieved 17 per cent of the global market, but its decline outpaced its swift growth. Today there is not a mill chimney left. Each remaining mill, a relic of strictly functional Victorian architecture (*both pictures*, upper left and top), shelters numerous industries – electronics, engineering, rainwear, wallpaper – but its upper floors are vacant or partly demolished.

If Oldham were in southern England it would be an important city and its 200,000 inhabitants might lead different lives. Here it is Greater Manchester's inglorious hanger-on. It has cleaner air and more open spaces; also deserts of waste ground (*new picture*, right and upper left) which could become oases of greenery but are more likely to end up as parking lots. This is post-industrial Lancashire, which seemed to Sir Kenneth Clarke to exemplify a nation's spiritual bankruptcy. There was more romance about in the smoky Oldham of times gone by, when another painter, not Lowry but Whistler, noted how the mills 'lost themselves in the dim sky, and the tall chimneys became *campanili*, and the warehouses of Oldham were palaces in the night'.

1955

Tonypandy

The South Wales valleys have been called a storm centre of geology – a confusion of the old red sandstone of Brecon with coal-bearing limestone ridges. Before the exploitation of minerals and the promiscuous spread of mining villages, it must have been spectacular country. Tonypandy is one of 22 villages in the two Rhondda valleys, where cramped but solidly-built cottages in long rows cling to the escarpments and every street disappears over a slope a few yards ahead of you. At the date of the *old picture*, the valley had 50 coalmines (the big local pit was at Llwynypia, top right of both *pictures*) – but since June 1986 no coal has been brought out of the Rhondda.

The *new picture* indicates, superficially, a happier place: clean air, where once 'even the snow was black'. But industry is dead and the community has disintegrated. "I was appalled," writes Lord Tonypandy (George Thomas, the former Commons Speaker), "to see how even the old Central Hall, founded by my grandfather and his generation, had been vandalised, and all the windows broken." The Methodist Central Hall (*old picture*, upper centre left, near river bridge) has made way for a small shopping centre (*new picture*, above new white bridge).

'How Green was my Valley' sang Richard Llewellyn, lamenting a
Rhondda from which industry had stripped the trees and grass and
had sown slag-heaps and ponds of brackish mine-water around. His
contemporaries saw cottages built within yards of pit tops, back doors
abutting on coke ovens, infant mortality become a national scandal;
and heard colliery owners telling select committees that "you often
find cocks and hens kept in their baths" and "if you give them a roomy
house, two families move into it."

There are houses to spare in Tonypandy now – empty, abandoned
and boarded-up. But material degeneration may open a way to
positive renewal, with a little encouragement from nature. Slag-heaps
have been reclaimed and landscaped (*new picture*, centre left),
vegetation has recovered its foothold (upper right) and heather and
yellow broom do well on shale. Healthy young chestnut trees may be
seen grappling with gritty slopes. Brackish ponds can become
ornamental pools (*both pictures*, lower left) or the reed-fringed haunts
of wildfowl. Some large ponds in blossoming leisure parks are
scheduled for watersports. Time will tell how green the valleys may be
and how soon the primroses will take root again on Primrose Hill in
Tonypandy – the name, incidentally, means 'splash of the watermill'.

1930

Immingham

The marshalling yards of the *old picture* (foreground), chock-full of coal trucks, and the coal conveyors to the basin where the colliers are lying (right of centre), recall an age of full employment in the Yorks, Notts and Derby coalfields and huge exports to London and the Continent. Nestling amid the coal dust, on the left of the entrance lock, is the small shipyard of the Humber Graving Dock. In World War II it refitted many Royal Navy destroyers.

Since 1969 the port area has been vastly enlarged, but the dock itself retains its original shape and size (*new picture*, upper right). Note the factories' capacious, well-filled car parks; the offshore loading jetties (top left and top right); the clusters of storage tanks of various types; and the new roads. The dual carriageway (bottom right) is an extension of the M180 motorway.

In times gone by, all the railway companies raced for a toe-hold on the coast. Thus Immingham came into existence: custom-built in 1912 by the Great Central line as a deep-water port for coal shipments. Sailors instructed to join ships at Immingham had to consult the gazetteer to find out where it was. Having found it – near the Humber

mouth, where the current swings close to the south bank – they discovered that it was almost impossible to reach. The best way was to make for Grimsby and scramble for a slatted wooden seat in the tram which carried the shunters and coal-heavers back and forth, taking 40 minutes for a seven-mile trip through fields. The terminus was to the right of the factory in the *old picture*, upper right.

Immingham is now on the map. Ships of weird and wonderful design come to the jetties – tankers and bulk carriers of strange and often dangerous cargoes. All the marsh country to the north-west (left of *both pictures*) is a 'special industries' zone, reserved for delicate and hazardous operations in the production of petro-chemicals and gas. Jet, Total and Petrofina petrols are refined here. Through Immingham the Conoco subsidiary of the chemicals giant Du Pont exports gas oils, kerosene, propane, butane and petroleum coke. Along the deepwater channel Calor Gas are excavating caverns for storing butane from North Sea gas. Complex distillates and all sorts of metals, minerals and chemicals come and go. But the conveyors are gone from the coaling berths, and a coal truck is a rare sight.

1934

Heysham

When the *Manxman* slid away from Platform 12 at Euston station someone reading the destination labels as they flicked past was bound to ask: "Where *is* Heysham?" Nowadays, thanks to the nuclear programme, Heysham is a more familiar name. The one-time port of embarkation (*old picture*) for Ireland and the Isle of Man is overshadowed by the square towers, big as blocks of flats, of Britain's largest and latest nuclear power complex. It has brought new residents to the undistinguished harbour town (*new picture*, upper right). What with that, and the southward expansion of the holiday resort of Morecambe, the two towns have virtually joined hands with each other, and with Lancaster five miles inland.

When Heysham was a man-made haven and a breakwater (extreme left), a rail terminus (upper right) and very little else, the black-and-white boats of the Isle of Man Steam Packet Company with the golden three-legged emblem on their red house flags sailed the short-sea route to Douglas, a 35-mile trip, and to Belfast in Northern Ireland. Three of the boats are visible in harbour in the *old picture*.

Twice a day the boat train pulled in and pulled out again, inspiring a brief period of waterfront bustle. Then all was quiet once more. It was the sort of place Pasternak might have had in mind when he wrote of 'the skyline of departures ending the history of situations'.

When the Central Electricity Generating Board chose Heysham for the site of a nuclear plant, the industry had passed nearly a century of milestones. In 1878 electricity illuminated a football match at Bramall Lane, Sheffield. Three years later the streets of Godalming in Surrey were electrically lit from power generated by the River Wey. By 1890 the electricity authorities were selling flat irons, fans and immersion heaters, and by 1918 cookers, vacuum cleaners and refrigerators.

In 1932 Cockcroft and Watson lifted energy into a new dimension by splitting the atom. The United States built the first nuclear reactor during World War II and Britain built the second in 1948. The world's first large-scale nuclear power station, at Calder Hall in Cumbria, went into action in 1956. The first commercial plants, at Berkeley and Bradwell, were commissioned in 1962.

The Heysham station, soon to be known as Heysham No. 1 (*new picture*, centre left, yellow rectangle), of the advanced gas-cooled reactor type, was begun in 1969 and completed in 1981. It cost £602 millions and was designed to supply the electricity needs of 2½ million people in the C.E.G.B.'s North-Western Region – three times the population of Manchester.

Heysham No. 2 (*new picture*, centre, white canopy above reactors) has been building since 1979 and its electricity is expected to start flowing into the national grid in 1989. It, too, is of the advanced gas-cooled type – the fifth in Britain – and will eventually, like No. 1, generate 1,320 megawatts.

Heysham No. 1 is open to visitors. The guided tour (no children) takes two hours. You can inspect the reactor from a viewing gallery and study an array of exhibition material. Those who prefer not to go quite so close may view the two plants from an observation tower (right of centre, in woods above the road).

Caravanners flock to the low shores and sandflats of the north Lancashire coast (*new picture*, extreme right), despite the proximity of the nuclear stations and the fact that the Irish Sea is supposed to have serious pollution problems. The harbour has never been enlarged, but it is deeper and is furnished with roll-on-roll-off facilities. The old Steam Packet Company has deserted Heysham, but its sister company, Manx Line, still runs a daily service to Douglas, Isle of Man. Returning, on a blustery evening, you have an almost surrealist view of your destination. Clouds mass over the lakeland fells (*new picture*, top), a setting sun lights up the stark wall of the Pennines directly ahead and the boiler towers, reactors and turbine and generator houses of Heysham Nos. 1 and 2, rising against a backdrop of hills, assume the shape of things to come.

1960

Greenock

Old picture: The sleek little vessel (bottom centre) identifies the shipyard as Scott's of Greenock, the submarine specialists. The yard is also busy with cargo carriers. Only one slipway appears to be vacant. Several harbour tugs lie at their berths in the Great Harbour (top centre) and James Watt Dock (upper centre right), ready to take the freighters out and bring others in. There are fishing boats too: Greenock was once an important herring port.

In our *new picture* it is high water. Docks and tidal basins are more pleasing to the eye, but not to the shipbuilder's eye. The cranes stand idle. The 'symphony of the Clyde' – more prosaically described by those who heard it as 'a helluva bashing din' – is now a funeral march, with plenty of rests. On the slipways nothing is being built, nothing repaired. The only vessel of any significance

is the red lightship in the basin (bottom centre right) – and she may be there for de-storing and de-commissioning, for lightships too are a dying breed.

Scott's of Greenock sank their identity when the historic Clyde yards – John Brown, Fairfield, Barclay Curle and others – underwent rationalization during shipbuilding's post-1950s slump. It became Scott Lithgow (Lower Clyde Shipbuilders), based on Port Glasgow (*both pictures*, top right) and Greenock. Great liners and warships came no more to these yards, but off-shore oil rigs kept a dwindling work force occupied. That kind of work is now virtually at an end. In October 1987, when Scott Lithgow announced a further 1,000 redundancies, the only order on the horizon – a tentative one – was for a small floating pier.

1961

Greenock: Container Port

Tall 'lands' or tenements (*old picture*, left centre), reminiscent of a Dutch or Belgian seaport, are not so concentrated now, but they are still the dominant architectural feature (*new picture*) of this grim Clydeside town. Discoloration in the water (*old picture*, top) reveals the Tail o' the Bank, a famous anchorage throughout 200 years of Greenock's history, memorable for its convoy assemblies in World War II. But the chief interest in our *pictures* lies in the in-filling of Albert Harbour where, apart from tiny craft, the only boat is a fishery protection vessel (*old picture*, upper left) and where the construction of a broad container quay subsequently cleared the waterfront as far as

the port authority buildings (*new picture*, upper centre). The quay is not exactly a hive of activity, any more than the old harbour was. Greenock's glory as a major port departed ages ago, when they deepened the Clyde and enabled big ships to sail into the heart of Glasgow.

The place has had its maritime moments. When local boy James Watt was still alive, in 1812, the world's first steamship service operated from Greenock: the 3½ horse power *Comet* to Glasgow, with room for 12 passengers beside the skipper, engineer and bagpiper. Their turnaround point (extreme right of the *old picture*) is still called the Steamboat Pier and was well known to

paddle-boat excursionists down the Clyde in pre-war days.

Extreme left of the waterfront in *both pictures* is Prince's Pier, the principal landing-stage. In olden days a genuine ocean terminal, it has in recent years served no destination more glamorous than Helensburgh, six miles across the water (*new picture*, extreme top left). Rocked, like most of Greenock, by two nights of devastating air raids in 1940, it bore for the next five years the warning:

THIS PIER IS COMPLETELY CLOSED TO THE
PUBLIC AND ALL ENTRY UNDER ANY
CIRCUMSTANCES IS EXPRESSLY FORBIDDEN.
BOOKSTALL ON PIER OPEN AS USUAL.

1920

Cheltenham

Advice to motorists from *The Autocar*, circa 1920: 'Once a week get your man to run his hand under the cylinder block. If his glove shows grease, sack the fellow instantly.' In those happy days, the *concours d'élégance* of vehicles and the immaculate tunics and polished gaiters of the chauffeurs at Cheltenham racecourse were an attraction second only to the horses. Vehicles in the course car park, and streaming along the road from Cheltenham (*old picture*, upper right to left), ranged from Rover, Jowett and Citroën coupés (£230 ex. works) to opulent 20-h.p. Crossleys and Armstrong-Siddeleys (£600) and Rolls Royces (£1,150). Motoring journals said you could run a car on a salary of £450 a year – which ruled out 95 per cent of the population.

This is Gold Cup week (*old picture*). The racecourse (top left, beyond ornate old grandstand), most fashionable of National Hunt venues, will always be associated with Fred Archer, the local innkeeper's son, 1857-1886. He rode 2,046 winners in his short life, was champion jockey 11 times in a row and then, having weight problems, committed suicide.

The *new picture* shows the neat new grandstand opposite the finish (centre right), the paddock, stables and administrative buildings of modern design. There is no racing this week. Traffic is confined to owners' and trainers' horse-boxes, cars and caravans. In summer the pantechnicons of commerce and leisure will take over: the site is used for trade fairs and various open-air events. New motorways and an airport have brought both tourism and business to the Regency town of Cheltenham, two miles south. Industries, however, are of a relatively genteel kind: hydraulic lifts, weighing machines, clocks and watches, interior furnishings and fire engines.

1965

Guildford

In 1928, just after Guildford had achieved diocesan status, a pious landowner gave six acres for a cathedral on Stag Hill (*old picture*, foreground). This was long before speculative builders had begun to nibble at the slopes. Seven years later, despite arguments over a design considered 'too severe', the cathedral foundations were laid. Interrupted by war, the building was not completed until 1961.

Guildford's population had greatly increased. The bypass roads laid out in the 1930s (*old picture*, top left) needed bypasses of their own. A tide of suburban housing was creeping round the hill into Guildford Park (*new picture*, foreground) and washing over Woodbridge Road to the railway (*old picture*, top left). On the south side, having trampled the sacred turf of the green belt – this is a ridge of the North Downs – property developers were pushing upward among the trees to within 50 yards of the cathedral itself.

Only the north front of the building, facing open parkland and pasture, gave a proper impression of tranquillity and detachment from secular affairs. And that was not for long. In 1966, work began on the University of Surrey and within two years hundreds of students were in residence.

Like Guildford itself, the University has now expanded to fill up more space than was originally allotted to it. The cathedral has battled to hold on to its six acres of hallowed ground, but houses, chiefly of the diocesan clergy and staff, have invaded the precincts (*new picture*, bottom right). Screens of planted cypresses and flowering trees (lower centre and right) are at present poor substitutes for a cathedral close.

Only the second English cathedral for 700 years to be built on a new site, the Cathedral of the Holy Spirit at Guildford is still perhaps too new to inspire lofty thoughts, but it does have a lofty site and is the Downs' most prominent landmark.

1932

Beaulieu

Beaulieu in our *old picture* was 'a strange, lonely place' (H.V. Morton, *In Search of England*) – a feudal village of thatched houses and an estate in severe financial difficulties. It has since prospered, under heavy tourist pressure.

The by-pass (foreground) relieves congestion among houses many of whose thatched roofs are gone, along with a serenity that only older inhabitants remember. The cottage allotments are a car park for the ambitious new village hall (lower centre), and gift shops abound.

Traffic chaos reached its height in the 1960s, when visitors to the Motor Museum were funnelled down the main street and through the entrance gates of Palace House (centre). But the National Motor Museum complex ('The Finest Day's Outing in the South') is now sited at a discreet distance, partly visible at the top left-hand corner of the *new picture*.

The highest saltwater reach of the Beaulieu River (*old picture*, centre right) presents a different scene in the *new picture* – it is high tide in the Solent.

Palace House, residence of the Montagus, was built round the gatehouse of a huge Cistercian abbey (1246) of which the cloisters survive (near red roof, above the house). The motoring connection started with the 2nd Lord Montagu, a horseless-carriage pioneer who recommended Daimler to King Edward VII – and a Daimler has been the royal car ever since. Maybe he would deplore the tourist trap which his son has planted at Beaulieu, but at least it has brought employment and restored the family fortune.

1959

Holme Pierrepont

Three miles east of Nottingham, the River Trent winds across strata of sand and gravel. From sand and gravel pits like those in the *old picture* upper right, one Nottingham company alone supplied ten per cent of Britain's needs. In 1958 deeper excavations began on the river bank (bottom left); sluices were installed (centre left); and the County Council and National Sports Council together created the Holme Pierrepont multi-watersports centre out of a string of stagnant pits. It cost £1½ million and it was opened in 1973.

The Trent flows across our *new picture* from bottom right to upper left, then curves back to top centre and the village of Radcliffe on Trent. An embankment separates the curve from the end of the Olympic rowing course (upper left to centre right), a rectangle of still water 12 feet deep, 150 yards wide and 1¼ miles long. The World Rowing championships were held here in 1986. Adjacent pools and lagoons and the river itself are used for dinghy and power-boat racing, water-skiing and angling. White-water canoeing and slalom are a recent addition (centre right).

Every summer weekend sees some kind of race or regatta in progress and August Bank Holiday is the day for the most spectacular professional events. But there are opportunities for recreation too. A 270-acre country park with camp sites, picnic areas and nature trails overlooks the whole scene. Note how the dreary pits and sand-spits of old have been smoothed out and sculpted to make a beautiful pleasure-ground: once a blot on the landscape, they now add life and colour.

Holme Pierrepont is still spreading its wings, and not only its water-wings. The aquatics are to be complemented with land-based activities: a football ground, a dog track, a show-jumping arena and a cycling stadium (Nottingham is the home of Raleigh bicycles). It could be years before all this comes to fruition but, if it does, what was years ago one of the most boring reaches of the Trent will have the largest and liveliest spectrum of sport and leisure in the whole of Britain. Meantime, at the water's edge, some new enticement – flower show, disco – is added every season.

1932

Aviemore

The views look south along the Spey (*both pictures*, upper left), with the Cairngorm foothills partly visible (top left), and portray the transformation of a quiet Highland village into a major winter-sports resort, the most extensive in Britain.

The Great North Road through Aviemore was still partly gravelled at the date of our *old picture* and the village looked much as it was 60 years earlier when Queen Victoria described it in her Journal as 'isolated, consisting of a general shop, a post office, a few cottages and an ancient inn.' The *Badenoch Record* of September 1932 noted that 'motor car traffic increases, and it is no uncommon thing to see a sleeping caravan drawn up beside a loch' – but the high point of the day came around 7am, when the Edinburgh-Inverness train set down a few passengers, mostly Englishmen making for their shooting tenancies and their fishing beats along the Spey.

About that time, a man carrying skis disembarked from the train.

The station-master asked: 'What are those planks for?' Thirty years later there were downhill runs from the bare tops above Rothiemurchus Forest (top left) and an Austrian ski school in the village. Major developments followed. Improved roads and new by-pass roads (*new picture*, right) now pierce the valley. Spurs go off at large roundabouts to the ski-tows at places formerly accessible only on dirt tracks. Along the flat flood plain of the Spey some 18 hotels, including Stakis, Post House and Ladbroke establishments, several mountaineer and ski schools and a great sports, leisure and conference centre (*new picture*, upper centre) stand on what used to be rough grazing ground and thin crofting strips (*old picture*, bottom).
On the Cairngorm slopes there are seven ski-tows and two chair-lifts, one of them ascending to Britain's highest restaurant, the Ptarmigan, at 3,600 feet.

Gleneagles Hotel

Most opulent of Scottish caravanserais, modelled on a French royal château with parterres and grass tennis courts (*both pictures*, centre right), Gleneagles Hotel has changed little in appearance, style or clientele. But it has put up its prices – 11 guineas a week in 1930, £100 plus per night now – and clothed its environment. The variegated woodland and shrubberies judiciously planted in the *old picture* (foreground) have reached maturity, giving protection from Perthshire's breezes to the latest of the hotel's four 18-hole golf courses (*new picture*, foreground). Behind, on the bleak Muir of Orchill (top), the ubiquitous conifers have gained a foothold. All over the central Highlands, dark blocks and dense screens of fir trees are invading the wild and romantic moorlands. Evidently they have their economic or ecological advantages, or the Forestry Commission would not be so fond of them. But the sight of their stiff phalanxes drawn up on the hillsides is usually disagreeable, especially to those who remember the Perthshire countryside of half a century ago – silver birches in the hollows, acres of oak and beech all aflame in the autumn sunshine, vast sheets of purple heather.

Perhaps familiarity will breed affection for the conifer plantations: Wordsworth protested vigorously against the larch, but two centuries later the larches which the Duke of Atholl planted at Dunkeld, a few miles from Gleneagles, are generally admired. And perhaps another generation will accept the conifers, having nothing to compare them with. Broadleaf plantings in Scotland are now only one per cent of the whole; and the area covered by conifers since 1945 has increased from 400 to more than 2,000 square miles. Apart from considerations of scenery, the loss to wildlife is incalculable.

Gleneagles Hotel (journalists who omit the word 'hotel' receive indignant letters from a neighbouring landowner whose house is properly called Gleneagles) was designed as the flagship of the prestige establishments of the railway companies when they first opened up the Highlands to well-heeled, salmon-fishing, deer-stalking, grouse-shooting visitors. The hotel has thrown open its doors to conferences, and recent additions include a shopping arcade, a golf school and a leisure centre. A private helipad has been added to the private railway station, to which first-class 'Gleneagles' sleepers once came from London.

1928

Crystal Palace

No structure more satisfying to London pride (with the possible exception of Tower Bridge) appeared throughout that ambitious building era, the Victorian age. No addition to the London skyline was more delighted in. The *old picture* shows the handsome site on Sydenham Hill, almost clear of the leafy outer suburbs, where 200 acres of landscaped gardens rose in shallow tiers to an architectural extravaganza moulded out of half a million panes of glass. The designer, horticulturist Joseph Paxton, permitted not a single brick or stone to be used. The result was a glittering palace, visible many miles away, lightly poised on its hilltop, an astonishing contrast to the solid magnificence of contemporary public monuments and buildings.

It was built to enshrine the Prince Consort's dream of a Grand Universal Exhibition promoting the 'happiness and brotherhood' of mankind. The Exhibition duly took place (1851) and during its five-

month run it attracted more than six million visitors. At any one time the Crystal Palace could accommodate 93,000 of them under its roof. Only the sparrows struck a jarring note: there were 93,000 of them too, beating their wings against the glass. There seemed no answer to the sparrow problem until Queen Victoria mentioned it to 82-year-old Wellington, the Iron Duke, and got the prompt reply: "Sparrow-hawks, ma'am".

By the date of our *old picture* the Palace was London's principal leisure centre. It had the tallest fountains and the loudest organ in the world. It was the venue for orchestral concerts, band competitions, revivalist meetings, political rallies and trade fairs. Blondin wheeled his barrow over the glass roofs on a tightrope stretched from tower to tower. For 20 years (1894-1914) they played the F.A. Cup Final at the Crystal Palace stadium. In the First World War it was a naval training 'ship', H.M.S. *Crystal Palace*. Early in the 1920s it acquired a speedway circuit and, in the South Tower, the first primitive television transmitter. Its fireworks displays were renowned all over Europe.

The biggest fireworks display occurred on 30th November 1936. The Palace went up in a blaze which all London's fire brigades fought in vain. The flames could be seen from the Downs near Brighton. Today (*new picture*) houses of Upper Norwood scamper over the hill like flocks of frightened sheep, but the Palace's general layout and terraces are still recognizable. The rebuilding plan has been shelved. The site is an athletics arena, staging important international events.

1921

Wembley

The *old picture*, facing page, might be a neolithic site, a girdle of standing stones and a vast tumulus. In fact it is a landscape in process of transformation: levelling, pillars for a concrete bowl and (foreground) designs for tree-planting.

Villagers of Wembley had their rustic seclusion disturbed in 1832 when navvies cut the route of the London & Birmingham railway. Thereafter little changed until the date of our picture, when the site was prepared for the British Empire Exhibition of 1924. London had had such exhibitions before, celebrations of imperial solidarity, acts of faith in the future of a global family on which the sun never set; and had splendid arenas for them too: Crystal Palace and White City, Earl's Court and Olympia. But this one required 200 acres, and the choice fell on Wembley, nine miles from central London. Trade fair pavilions and fairground amusements spread over the fields, displaying, it was said, the best architecture seen in Britain this century. The Malaya Building (striped minarets) and the Palace of India (a Taj Mahal look-alike) were especially admired. All the buildings afterwards came down and suburban houses and factories (*new picture* top right) went up.

Seventeen million people tramped across Wembley between May and October 1924 – a world record for exhibition attendance. Most found their way into the 16-acre centre-piece, the biggest stadium ever built, for Pageants of Empire, Exhibition Rodeos and Military Torchlight Tattoos.

Scarcely a trace of the great Exhibition remains; not much of Wembley village as it was, either. But the stadium became the arena for important international football matches and for England's domestic Cup Finals, in the first of which (April 1923) Bolton Wanderers beat West Ham two-nil. Costly improvements of recent years have given Wembley Stadium a fully-covered seating capacity of 100,000. Big multiple stores and one of the nation's largest DIY emporia (top centre, top left) line Wembley Way, the avenue on which the fans approach, which comes in upper left to the twin towers of the main entrance. There is a colossal hotel (centre left) and the huge Wembley Pool built in 1934 for Olympic events. Now known as Wembley Arena, 240 feet from floor to ceiling, it is used for ice shows and show jumping. All this and speedway track, greyhound track and conference centre make this corner of north London a metropolis of entertainment.

Wembley, across the tracks (bottom right), tries to remain aloof. Greater London has swallowed much of the district. There was a period in the 1960s when, because traffic jams had brought the City to a standstill, no further office development was permitted there; and Wembley emerged as the favourite alternative. The most extravagant development, around Wembley Stadium, has preserved the greenest and most spacious environment.

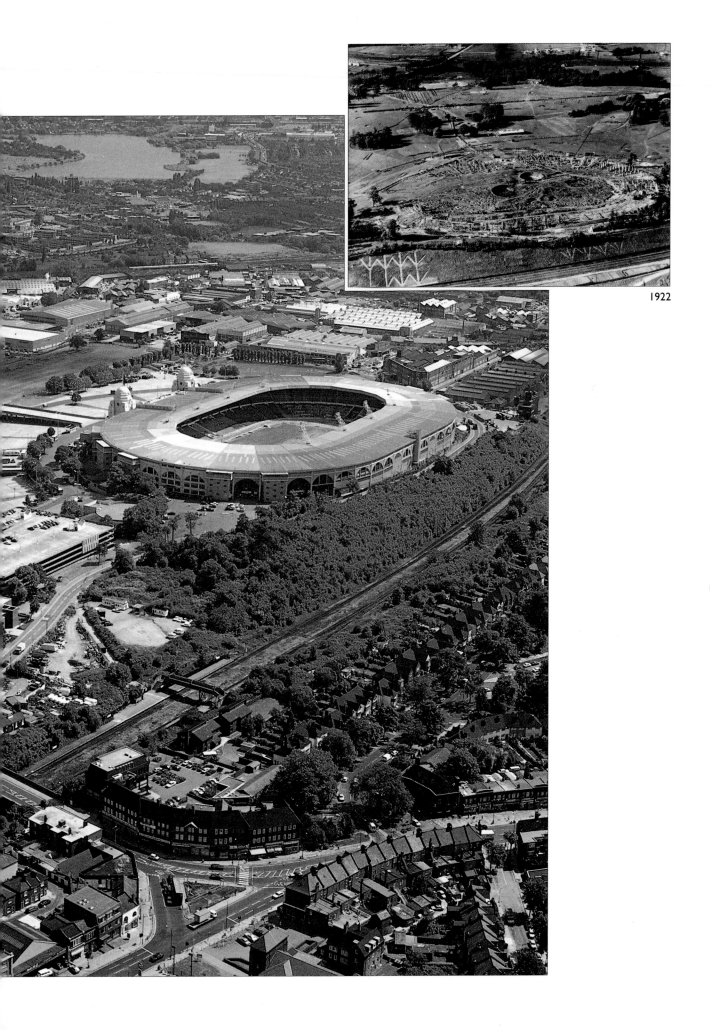

1922

1937

Plymouth

"All the nice girls love a sailor" – you can almost hear the strains floating up from the pier pavillion under Plymouth Hoe (*old picture*, foreground). It was the heyday of the West Country port, of girls in Kiss-Me-Quick hats and of Jack ashore from the warships in Devonport dockyard. Pier and bandstand went long ago to the scrapyard. Hoe Road (*new picture*, foreground) is a clean corniche with uninterrupted views down Plymouth Sound. All the city centre (*new picture*, centre left) is modern. In eleven nights in spring 1941, air raids killed 1,000 people and wrecked 30,000 buildings. On a traffic island behind the bus station (upper left, near head of inlet) the ruin of Charles Church is preserved as a reminder of the horrors of war. The new shops and offices on Royal Parade and Armada Way (extreme left) are not remarkable, but the new Guildhall and Civic Centre (left of Drake's refurbished statue, centre left) are worthy of this city's proud heritage. On the Hoe itself the bandstand and the deck-chaired crowds it attracted (*old picture*, centre) are no more, but the lighthouse, locally as famous as the Eddystone 15 miles beyond the Sound, stands firm, hooped with red as the laws of the sea nowadays prescribe.

Sprawled over the estuaries of the Rivers Plym (top), Tavy, Tamar, Limber and Tiddy, the city owed much to its deep-water inlets and the seafaring traditions built up by Devon's merchant adventurers, notably Francis Drake its one-time mayor. The oldest quarter is the Barbican, the sea inlet (upper right to upper centre) where New Street – new when the Armada sailed by – has its original cobbles. Here the Pilgrim Fathers set sail in 1620. On its western edge the 17th-century Citadel (*both pictures*, centre right), knocked about in 1941, afterwards sensitively restored, was once acknowledged to be Europe's finest military stronghold. When it was new, a chronicler described the Barbican and its doubly-landlocked inner harbour of Sutton as 'a mene thing, an habitation of fishars'. The clusters of yachts and motor-boats at the marinas (*new picture*, centre right and upper centre) indicate that leisure cruising and water-sports are the growth industries around Plymouth and its inlets these days and that if we meet with any 'fishars' they will probably be down here for a sea-angling holiday.

1926

Hyde Park Corner

Green Park (*both pictures*, right) and Hyde Park (left, with sandy strip of Rotten Row) are little changed. Waves of new construction beat in vain against the capital's cherished parks, the envy of great foreign cities. As the saying goes, you may still walk across London on grass.

Today there are startling changes in the styles, heights and density of the buildings around Hyde Park Corner which make it the architectural counterpart of the City around St Paul's. But these are mostly super de luxe multi-bedroom hotels, all jostling for elbow room along Knightsbridge (*new picture* lower centre left), Piccadilly (centre to upper right) and Park Lane (centre to upper left). They include, extreme left, the new Berkeley; on Piccadilly, the Athenaeum and Park Lane; on Park Lane itself, the huge Intercontinental, the Inn on the Park and the towering Hilton. What the Queen thinks of strangers with binoculars peering into her private gardens (lower right) from the upper floors can only be guessed at.

The senior hotel, the Dorchester, which replaced Dorchester House in 1931 (*both pictures*, top left), looks dowdy by comparison. Beige-coloured Apsley House – 'No. 1, Piccadilly', the Duke of Wellington's house – in centre of the *new picture* is dwarfed by the Intercontinental across the street. On the new large traffic island the old landmarks of Artillery monument, Wellington statue and Wellington Arch at the end of Constitution Hill look suddenly inconspicuous.

South of Knightsbridge (*both pictures*, lower left), next to St George's hospital on the Corner, is the site of the Alexandra hotel, destroyed in a 1941 air raid. It is now occupied by Agriculture House, the rather overpowering N.F.U. headquarters.

'It is calculated that 300 stage-coaches pass through Hyde Park Corner daily,' said a newspaper of 1824. A century later it was 50,000 motor vehicles – not many fewer than today, because (despite an increase in volume) since 1963 the Knightsbridge-Piccadilly underpass has diverted much traffic beneath this notorious bottleneck.

1957

1961

Severn Bridge

Many people who came from the north on childhood holidays to the south-west will remember with affection the Beachley-Aust ferry across the Severn; it was the highlight of the journey. The forest fleece of the Wye valley petered out miserably in a canyon of mud under the walls of Chepstow (*old picture*, top centre). Then came the short steep descent to the boat, which loaded six cars and took a wide sweep in a ripping current and delivered you to the Aust ferry-slip in 15 minutes. You rarely waited in a queue of vehicles. Though it saved a 60-mile detour through Gloucester, it was not a heavily-trafficked crossing.

Since 1966 the Severn suspension bridge (*interim* and *new pictures*) has connected the same two points, Beachley and Aust. Traffic has increased enormously, for the bridge carries the M4 motorway which links the Chiswick flyover in London with the mountains of Dyfed 200 miles away; and in the holiday rush it can still take 15 minutes to cross the narrows. It may be that a few years hence the aerial panorama will show two road bridges, the planners having suggested that one is not really enough. On this bridge, which is 2½ miles long and leaps over the Wye (top) as well as the Severn, motorists pay a toll (*new picture*, toll bridge left foreground). But from the car parks on the southern approaches (centre foreground) you can reach the footway and cycle path (left side of bridge) and walk or pedal from Somerset to Monmouthshire. Or you might climb down Aust Cliff (*new picture*, centre left) and hunt for fossils on the 'bone beds', where not long ago a boy found an ichthyosaurus's jawbone and teeth.

The new Severn Bridge is the second of that name. Its Victorian predecessor, a railway viaduct ten miles upstream at Sharpness, was dismantled in 1957.

1948

Radlett

There is really no comparison. The freight trains of the *old picture*, for all their sound and fury, their smelly smoke and midnight clanking, might take a week to deliver a consignment from London to Manchester. (They called them 'fast goods'.) The electric four-coach commuter train of the *new picture* is speedy, silent, efficient and comfortable.

Steam buffs, however, deplore the workman-like simplicity of the present-day freight trains, made up of scores of container trucks all exactly alike and travelling chiefly through the night; and the functional neatness of the passenger stock. They yearn for the heterogeneous collections (*old picture*, lower right) of coal wagons, cattle trucks, tankers, hoppers, timber wagons and multi-coloured vans all attached to one train which could be studied in many pages of the Hornby model railway catalogue and be seen lifesize at many a line-side vantage-point. They remember the bright liveries of the old-time passenger coaches, when the railway companies had their individual colours.

Our trains are photographed near Radlett (note how Borehamwood, lower left, has encroached on the scene), on the fastest stretch of the old Midland line from St Pancras. At the date of the *old picture*, the express trains were timed to cover the 99 miles to Leicester in 99 minutes, but already the L.M & S. railway was deep into the steam-versus-diesel debate. Something drastic had to be done, because the pre-war locomotives were worn out and between 1939 and 1946 no new ones had been built. The company ordered two diesels and built two *Pacific*-class steam locomotives to compete with them in speed and endurance trials. But nationalization overtook all the railway companies before that interesting experiment could be carried out.

Diesel trains first appeared in B.R.'s Eastern region; electrification proceeded fastest on southern routes. The last long-distance steam train left Paddington in 1975. But time has not diminished the nostalgia for steam. Enthusiasts continually bring old locomotives out of retirement to haul excursionists on renovated sections of abandoned track; and customers flock to board the trains.

1931

1946

Heathrow

The 'heath' of Heathrow was Hounslow Heath. Its dangerous cover, from which footpads and highwaymen emerged to gather rich pickings from travellers into London, had not entirely disappeared when the *old picture* was taken (copses and orchards along the A4, upper right to left). Modern travellers, paying inflated prices for short-haul tickets and duty-free purchases and occasionally finding their suitcases rifled into the bargain, have been heard to mutter that the old 'stand and deliver' techniques are not forgotten.

This was also brick-making country. Hounslow bricks built Hampton Court. Dickens drew on local colour for his sordid out-of-town slum scenes, as in *Bleak House*. Cobbett in the 1830s found Heathrow 'bad in soil and villainous in outlook' but, once the marshes

had been drained, market gardening flourished.

By the date of the *interim picture*, the skeleton of the great airport, designated as Croydon's replacement, had been laid down. It remained only to clothe the ribs with tarmac, concrete and a passenger terminal. By 1950 Heathrow was handling half a million travellers annually. But they all checked in at a caravan, and stood about in a marquee, and then walked out to their aircraft on duckboards, across wet grass.

The first permanent structure, Queen's Building (*new picture*, upper centre left), formed the nucleus of the main terminals, three in number, which were islanded in runways and approached via a road tunnel from the A4 (*new picture*, upper left). One by one the airport

hotels sprang up along the same road; nearly all the major hotel chains are represented in this area today.

The airport is the grand crossroads of the world's aerial routes, from East to West and from North to South. In numbers of flights and passengers handled, according to Civil Aviation Authority statistics, it has for the past 30 years dealt with almost twice as much traffic as its nearest European rivals – Frankfurt, Amsterdam and Paris Orly. It still holds the title of 'world's busiest airport' although since 1975 New York JFK has been steadily closing the gap.

Heathrow is now one vast industrial estate of depots, workshops, warehouses, hangars, offices, maintenance units, control posts and inter-connecting roads. It employs 55,000 workers. Recent developments have given the airport its own tube station, a direct link with central London; and a new passenger terminal, making four in all. The aircraft which sit quietly at their gates in the *new picture* convey no idea of the perpetual bustle, clamour and (to the innocent traveller) chaos of Heathrow. It is said that a flight of some sort – passenger, private or freight – lands or takes off every 15 seconds. On the left of the dark geometry of the sewage works (*new picture*, bottom right) is No. 1 runway, black with burned rubber. The bird's-eye view diminishes the scale: there is a 20-minute scheduled flight between two airports in the Orkney islands which is actually shorter in distance than this runway.

1955

Royal Dockland/London City Airport

The scenes are Dockland ancient and modern: journey's end for merchant seamen (*old picture*), a launching pad for city gents (*new*).

In its heyday, the cargo carriers and passenger liners, like exotic birds of passage, settled in flocks. They wore the flags of various nations and were attended by flotillas of lighters whose cumbersome, labour-intensive activities up and down the Port of London appear nowadays as curious as the traffic of medieval Venice. Yet the lighters handled half the imports and nearly a third of the exports of the whole of Britain.

The 'royal' group of docks in Newham on the north bank of the Thames consisted of the Royal Victoria (top right), the Royal Albert (centre right) and the King George V (centre left). Built in 1855, 1880 and 1921 respectively, they were the nation's largest area of dock water. Each was more than a mile long. They accommodated the biggest vessels afloat. In 1939 the *Mauretania* was refitted in the King George V dock.

The *new picture* shows a little more of the London river, which comes down by Woolwich Reach (upper left) and curves round the docks' entrance in Gallion's Reach. Across to Woolwich goes the free ferry (curving pier, extreme left) and across to Greenwich stride

the shiny scoops of the Thames Barrier, a spectacular flood control system installed in 1981 (top centre, left). Slum housing in Silvertown (*old picture* upper left) has been replaced by a refinery and some medium-and high-rise flats. Incomers from the higher income brackets will fill up the vacant spaces if the developers have their way. An inducement for some, a deterrent to others, is the short-take-off-and-landing ('stol') London city airport (*new airport* centre), the first 'stolport' in Europe. Built with City money and designed primarily for City use, this new transport base is seven miles from central London, compared with Heathrow's 15 and Gatwick's 28 – and you can park your car a few yards from the check-in desk. Jet aircraft, cosier and quieter than most, began in October 1987 to carry passengers and freight to Paris, Brussels and Amsterdam. A saving of up to 80 minutes on capital-to-capital flights is claimed.

On the minus side, fares are high; fog and mist disrupt winter schedules; and the neighbours are already complaining about the noise. Will the new airport prove itself, or will it end up as another few acres of derelict dockland, looking as strange and antiquated tomorrow as today does the old-time bustle of cargo boat, crane and lighter?

Index of Place Names